*George*

Wendy Cope was born in Kent, read history at Oxford and then worked for 15 years as a primary school teacher in London. She began writing poems in her spare time, and published her first collection, *Making Cocoa for Kingsley Amis*, in 1986. Since then she has been a freelance writer. A second collection of poems, *Serious Concerns*, appeared in 1992 and was followed by *If I Don't Know* in 2001. She has also written some poems for children and edited several anthologies, including *The Funny Side* (1998) and *Heaven on Earth: 101 Happy Poems* (2001). She lives in Winchester.

*The Golden Age
of Spiritual Writing*
Series editor: David Scott

Lancelot Andrewes: The Private Prayers
*Selected and translated by David Scott*

George Herbert: Verse and Prose
*Selected and introduced by Wendy Cope*

Thomas Traherne: Poetry and Prose
*Selected and introduced by Denise Inge*

*The Golden Age
of Spiritual Writing*

# George Herbert

## Verse and Prose

Selected and introduced by
Wendy Cope

Published in Great Britain in 2002 by
Society for Promoting Christian Knowledge
Holy Trinity Church
Marylebone Road
London NW1 4DU

Copyright © Wendy Cope 2002

All rights reserved. No part of this book may be reproduced or transmitted in any form or by any means, electronic or mechanical, including photocopying, recording, or by any information storage and retrieval system, without permission in writing from the publisher.

British Library Cataloguing-in-Publication Data
A catalogue record for this book is available from the British Library

ISBN 0-281-05475-4

10 9 8 7 6 5 4 3 2 1

Typeset by FiSH Books, London WC1
Printed in Great Britain by Antony Rowe Ltd, Chippenham, Wiltshire

# Contents

| | |
|---|---|
| The Golden Age of Spiritual Writing | ix |
| Introduction | xiii |
| A Note on Reading Herbert | xxvi |
| The Dedication | 1 |
| The Church-Porch | 2 |
| The Altar | 21 |
| The Reprisall | 22 |
| Redemption | 23 |
| Easter | 24 |
| Easter-Wings | 25 |
| Sinne | 26 |
| Affliction | 27 |
| Prayer | 30 |
| The Holy Communion (1) | 31 |
| Antiphon | 33 |
| Employment | 34 |
| The Holy Scriptures | 35 |
| Whitsunday | 36 |
| Mattens | 37 |
| Even-Song | 38 |
| Church-Musick | 39 |
| The Windows | 40 |
| Trinitie Sunday | 41 |
| Content | 42 |
| The Quidditie | 44 |
| Avarice | 45 |
| To all Angels and Saints | 46 |
| Deniall | 47 |
| Vertue | 48 |

| | |
|---|---|
| The Pearl | 49 |
| Unkindnesse | 51 |
| Life | 52 |
| Mortification | 53 |
| Jordan | 55 |
| Conscience | 56 |
| The British Church | 57 |
| The Quip | 58 |
| Dialogue | 59 |
| Providence | 60 |
| Sinnes Round | 66 |
| Peace | 67 |
| Mans Medley | 69 |
| The Storm | 71 |
| The Method | 72 |
| Divinitie | 74 |
| The Discharge | 75 |
| Praise | 77 |
| The Collar | 78 |
| The Glimpse | 79 |
| The Call | 80 |
| The Pulley | 81 |
| The Priesthood | 82 |
| The Search | 84 |
| Grief | 87 |
| The Crosse | 88 |
| The Flower | 90 |
| The Sonne | 92 |
| A True Hymne | 93 |
| Bitter-sweet | 94 |
| The Glance | 95 |
| The Forerunners | 96 |
| The Invitation | 98 |
| The Elixir | 100 |
| A Wreath | 101 |
| Judgement | 102 |

|   |   |
|---|---|
| Heaven | 103 |
| Love | 104 |
| From *A Priest to the Temple* or *The Country Parson* | |
|   The Parson praying | 105 |
| The Holy Communion (2) | 107 |
| Letter to Sir Henry Herbert | 109 |
| A Selection from *Outlandish Proverbs* | 111 |
| Select Bibliography | 115 |
| Index of First Lines | 117 |

# The Golden Age of Spiritual Writing

The Golden Age of Spiritual Writing brings together a series of books of English 'spiritual' poetry and prose, selected and introduced by well-known contemporary authors and scholars. Many of the writers on whom this series focuses flourished during the seventeenth century. You may well ask, 'Why concentrate on writers of the seventeenth century? Wasn't it a long time ago?' Historically, that period might well seem 'a long time ago', especially when we consider the huge changes in communications and in scientific understanding, and, yet, looked at with the long view of human history, the seventeenth century is quite recent. It was, in many ways, the beginning of the modern age. We share with the people of that time the struggles and strains of being human, the joys as well as the challenges of the natural world, and the seemingly incontrovertible facts of birth and death. In our religious lives, too, we want to talk about the challenges of new cultures bearing down on what we consider eternal truths, and the relationship between different Christian traditions.

But we do bother about the seventeenth-century writers, and have done with increasing enthusiasm since the early part of the twentieth century, with the name and influence of T. S. Eliot ranking large. I think we bother about them for three main reasons. First, they write well. Second, they tell eternal truths. And third, for our spiritually bewildered age, they fill a dry well with clear, fresh water.

There is something about the English language of this period that has an element of the miraculous. We find this most commonly in the plays of Shakespeare and in the Authorized Version of the Bible: the two books without which any stay on a desert island is deficient. Their language is not so removed from our own that we are utterly confused by it, but it is freshly coined enough to retain its life, its bite and chew. It has the power to evoke in us, physically, the moods, emotions and thoughts the words are trying to express. The words and the rhythms can make us cry and laugh and ponder with a huge intensity. Someone could probably explain this miracle and find it, for sure, in other writers of different ages; but all I want to do is to encourage readers to see if it is true for them about the seventeenth century. However, when it comes to dealing with the translated material of Lancelot Andrewes then different linguistic criteria have to be applied.

The words have to be about something. It is not just a matter of style or sound. The words have to tell us something that we find valuable. This series concentrates on spiritual writers. Each of them refers easily and unashamedly to God, and not infrequently to Jesus Christ as the revelation of God's love in and for the world. They write of sin and prayer, of salvation and love, of death and heaven and hell, and they mean real things by them. The writers precede the growth of rationalism that developed in the eighteenth century. Are we not too grown up and too clever for such things? Are we not, as Eliot put it, banging an antique drum? Each of the books in this series will be at pains to persuade us that this is not so, and more importantly, the writers themselves will do so, too. They take the great spiritual themes of all times and places: desire, fear, decision-making, a sense of wonder and of awe, anxiety and loss, and, by their own vision and breadth of experience, make them reach down to us in our own day.

Reading the great classics of spiritual literature of whatever age today will always be a new thing, it is a new generation that is reading them. Reading Traherne in an era of massive pollution will put his sense of wonder and affection for the natural world in a new political context. Donne's honesty about sex and religion will raise questions about the nature of humanity, which, after Freud, will seem as real as ever. Herbert's gentle, pragmatic ethics might encourage a new generation to reflect on standards of behaviour and the place of an ordered life in a free-floating world. Each of the writers presented in this series will have something to contribute to the contemporary debate. Pondering these questions will be to the benefit of both writer and reader. The echoes of great literature come not only from within the text itself, but also from outside the text. In reading the poetry, the thoughts, the prayers, we make them live again. For people searching for the words that express what they want to say, here in this series will be some familiar resources and, I trust, some revelations.

As editor of the series, I would like to thank all the authors who agreed to contribute. I am especially grateful for the high quality of their work, which has made my task so much easier. I have worked closely throughout with the editorial team at SPCK, especially with Liz Marsh. I am immensely grateful to them for their friendly support and for their decision to take on the publication of this fascinating area of spiritual writing. Without them this series would never have come together.

David Scott<br>
Winchester

# Introduction

Like many other people, I first came across the work of George Herbert very early in life. I sang it in church and school chapel, without noticing the name of the author. Many years later, as an adult with an interest in poetry, I bought a selection of Herbert's poems in a second-hand bookshop. It was a pleasant surprise to find that I already knew some of them almost by heart: 'The Elixir' ('Teach me, my God and King'), 'Praise' ('King of Glorie, King of Peace'), 'Antiphon' (Let all the world in ev'ry corner sing'). Nowadays I take care to look and see who wrote the words of the hymn we're singing.

Since I had never done Herbert in English lessons at school, most of his work was new to me. I took to it immediately. What especially appealed to me – and still does – was this poet's wonderfully playful delight in poetic form, and the fact that these playful poems are, at the same time, utterly serious. In our time there is a tendency to associate technical bravura with 'light verse'. Herbert is one of the poets who shows us that this need not be so. There is humour, as well as exuberant inventiveness, in his work, but no one challenges his standing as a serious poet, whose primary concern was not to show off but to tell the truth.

When I first read that second-hand book, I was not a churchgoer, and thought of myself as an atheist. Over the years critics have discussed whether or not one needs to be a Christian to appreciate Herbert's poems. I can answer this with absolute certainty: one does not. However, in the last eight years, since I began going to church again, I have grown still fonder of these poems, valuing them, to borrow a phrase from W. H. Auden, as 'expressions of Anglican piety at its best'.

In recent years I have also read about Herbert's life. The most famous account, Izaak Walton's *The Life of Mr George Herbert*, is a beautiful piece of writing that has been described as 'a classic of

Christian literature'. It is not now regarded as wholly reliable. The power of this work is one of the reasons why the story of Herbert's 'holy and exemplary life' has, at times, threatened to overshadow his reputation as a poet. In the last century, scholarly research resulted in some amendments to Walton's version, but the story is still an inspiring one.

## The life of George Herbert
George Herbert was born in Montgomery in 1593, 29 years after the birth of William Shakespeare and ten years before the death of Queen Elizabeth I. His father, Richard Herbert, was descended from the earls of Pembroke, his mother Magdalene (neé Newport) from the princes of Powys. The family was described by Herbert's friend Barnabas Oley as 'generous, noble and ancient'.

George was the seventh of ten children. When his father died in 1596, his mother was left with six boys and three girls and she was two months pregnant with the youngest child, Thomas. By all accounts Magdalene Herbert was a remarkable woman – strong, well-educated and devoutly religious. In 1597 she took her young family to live with her mother in Eyton-upon-Severn, and in 1599 moved with them to Oxford, where the eldest son Edward (later Lord Herbert of Cherbury) was a student. It was probably here that she first met John Donne, who became a good friend and continued to visit the family after the Herberts moved to London and set up home in Charing Cross in 1601.

Another close friend of the Herberts was Lancelot Andrewes, who was to be one of the translators of the King James Bible, Bishop of Chichester, of Ely and of Winchester, and author of sermons that are still read today. In 1601 Andrewes was installed Dean of Westminster, and may have taught George when he first entered Westminster School in 1604 or 1605, though Dean Andrewes moved on to Chichester in the latter year.

In the house at Charing Cross, Magdalene Herbert conducted prayers every morning and evening, and psalm-singing on Sunday evenings. She also attended a church service every day. But the family also enjoyed some more worldly pleasures, such as music-making, with George playing the lute and viol. George was a talented musician and music-lover, and there are many musical images in his poems. A more surprising family pastime – playing cards for money – may help to explain the last three words of his poem 'The Quidditie', 'most take all'. John Tobin, one of Herbert's editors, points out that this 'looks suspiciously like an expression used in card-playing'.

In 1609 Magdalene got married again, to a much younger man, Sir John Danvers. This seems to have caused some problems with Edward but not with the younger children. George's letters to Danvers are affectionate and respectful, and there is no evidence of hostility between them. In the same year George, who had been a hard-working and successful schoolboy, was admitted to Trinity College, Cambridge.

Here, too, he did well. Little is known about his course of study for his BA but in 1614, the year he took it, he was elected a minor fellow of Trinity, and in 1615 or 1616 a major fellow of the same college. By now he was studying classics and divinity for his MA, which he took in 1616. In 1618 Herbert was appointed to a university post, Praelector or Reader in Rhetoric.

These appointments helped somewhat to ease his financial situation. Richard Herbert had indicated in his will that each of his younger children should receive 40 pounds a year from their eldest brother, who inherited the estate. However, Edward cut the suggested amount to 30 pounds per annum and didn't always pay it on time.

The position improved further when Herbert was appointed in 1619 to the prestigious post of Public Orator of Cambridge University. He described his duties in a letter to his stepfather: '[the Orator] writes all the University Letters, makes all the Orations, be it to King, Prince, or whatever comes to the University.' Herbert now had good prospects of achieving high public office. It is possible that he had already met King James on one of his visits to Cambridge. He certainly came into contact with him now, and with powerful courtiers.

According to Walton, Herbert was at this time 'hoping, that as his predecessors, so he might in time attain the place of a Secretary of State'. However,

> God, in whom there is an unseen chain of causes, did in a short time put an end to the lives of his two most obliging and powerful friends, Lodowick, Duke of Richmond, and James, Marquess of Hamilton, and not long after him King James died also, and with them all Mr Herbert's court hopes.

It was as a result of this disappointment, says Walton, that Herbert, after a period of ill health and soul-searching, decided to 'enter into Sacred Orders'.

This simple narrative, with the sudden and dramatic change of plan after the king's death in 1625, is still widely accepted as a true account, even though it has been questioned by scholars for more than 50 years. The truth, it seems, is neither so clear, nor so simple. The biographer Amy Charles takes the view that, long before 1625, it was Herbert's intention to be ordained, and that he 'proceeded rather steadily in his study of divinity' from 1616 onwards.

In any case, there is ample evidence in Herbert's poems of a struggle with worldly ambition. It is possible that the prospect of secular preferment tempted him to abandon a long-term plan to go into the Church. The death of the king was probably not the only factor that influenced his decision. In 1623 he entered Parliament as member for the borough of Montgomery and, along with his friend Nicholas Ferrar, became involved in a conflict with the crown concerning a crisis in the affairs of the Virginia Company. After this Ferrar retired from the world to found the religious community at Little Gidding. Herbert may have experienced a similar disenchantment with public life.

We do not know exactly when Herbert was ordained deacon – a step that debarred him from civil employment – but it seems likely that the decision to do so had been made by the end of 1624 (before the death of King James). In 1626 he was installed by proxy a canon of Lincoln Cathedral and prebend of Leighton Ecclesia. His only duty as canon was to preach one sermon a year. The latter appointment did not involve any parish duties, as the parish already had its own vicar. He did, however, put a great deal of energy into raising funds for the rebuilding of the parish church.

Herbert, at the age of 33, was still not committed to any full-time employment. He took leave of absence from the oratorship in 1623 and gave up the position in 1628. He spent the years between 1624 and 1630 staying with friends and relations, suffering at least one bout of serious illness and, all biographers agree, thinking hard about his future.

Although little is known about the exact dates when Herbert wrote his poems, it was probably during this period that he composed 'Affliction':

> Now I am here, what thou wilt do with me
>           None of my books will show:
> I reade, and sigh, and wish I were a tree;
>           For sure then I should grow
> To fruit or shade: . . .

And 'Employment':

> All things are busie; onely I
> Neither bring hony with the bees,
> Nor flowres to make that, . . .

and expressed his doubts about his worthiness in 'The Priesthood'.

Herbert had been writing poems, in English and in Latin, since he was a teenager. At the beginning of 1610, aged 17, he sent his mother two Sonnets, together with a letter saying, 'my meaning (dear Mother) is in these Sonnets to declare my resolution to be, that my poor Abilities in Poetry, shall be all, and ever consecrated to God's glory.'

The long poem called 'The Church-Porch' is thought to have

been written as early as 1614, and may be addressed to Henry Herbert, the poet's favourite brother. There is reason to believe that many of the poems eventually included in Herbert's book *The Temple* were written before he settled at Bemerton for the last three years of his life. In the words of Joseph Summers, 'Before Herbert was ordained priest in 1630, he was already one of England's greatest religious poets.'

In 1627 Herbert's mother died. John Donne delivered a memorial sermon in her honour. The following year Sir John Danvers remarried. Herbert continued to have a good relationship with his stepfather and, for a time, lived with Danvers' older brother, the Earl of Danby, near Chippenham in Wiltshire. There he met and, in 1629, married Jane Danvers, a cousin of his stepfather. After the marriage the couple moved in with Jane's parents, who lived less than 20 miles away.

A year after his marriage, Herbert was offered full-time employment as a parish priest. He hesitated for a month before accepting the living of Fugglestone-with-Bemerton, near Salisbury. He was, at last, ordained priest at Salisbury Cathedral in September 1630, six months after being installed as rector. At this point in his narrative Izaak Walton tells the reader 'to prepare for an almost incredible story of the great sanctity of the short remainder of his holy life'.

There seems to be no doubt at all that Herbert was a very good parish priest – devout, conscientious and kind. His brother Edward, writing a decade after George's death, says this:

> his life was most holy and exemplary, in so much that about Salisbury... he was little less than sainted. He was not exempt from passion and choler, being infirmities to which all our race is subject, but that excepted, without reproach in his actions.

The little church of St Andrew at Bemerton still stands today, on a traffic island in a suburb of Salisbury. Across the road is the same rectory that Herbert occupied. The River Nadder runs at the bottom of the garden. Twice a week, Herbert walked along the riverside to Salisbury Cathedral to hear sung evensong, an experience he described as his 'Heaven upon earth'.

After a lifetime of ill health, Herbert died in Bemerton rectory on 1 March 1633, aged 39, and was buried in St Andrew's church two days later.

None of his English poems had appeared in print in his lifetime. When he was dying he arranged for his handwritten book of them to be taken to Nicholas Ferrar at Little Gidding with this message: 'if he think it may turn to the advantage of any dejected poor soul, let it be made public; if not, let him burn it.' By the end of 1633, *The Temple* was in print.

The book was an immediate success – four editions were published in three years. In the ensuing decades, Herbert's appeal extended across the religious divide that was soon to tear the nation apart. His work was admired by Anglicans (including King Charles) and by Puritans on both sides of the Atlantic. Numerous poets, of whom the most distinguished was Henry Vaughan, attempted to imitate him.

He was less highly regarded in the eighteenth century, and no new editions appeared between 1709 and 1799. In the nineteenth century, Herbert was championed by Coleridge and Ruskin and, in America, by Ralph Waldo Emerson. Opinion as to the value of his work continued to be divided until the 1930s, when T. S. Eliot made a very influential contribution to the debate, asserting that Herbert is 'a major poet'. Since then his reputation has gone from strength to strength. Three and a half centuries after his death, the poems of George Herbert look set to last 'so long as men can breathe, or eyes can see' (Shakespeare, Sonnet 18).

## *George Herbert's literary work*

The book that the dying Herbert sent to Nicholas Ferrar had three sections, entitled 'The Church-Porch', 'The Church' and 'The Church Militant' (which consists of one long poem in rhyming couplets, not included here). The overall title, *The Temple*, may not be Herbert's own.

The main body of his poetry is in the middle section, 'The Church'. Herbert arranged the poems in the order he wanted, with 'Love' (described by Simone Weil as *'le plus beau poème du monde'*) at the end. Most of Herbert's editors have left the order unchanged, and I have done the same except that, since this is a selection, there are poems missing.

The first section, like the third, consists of one long poem. It is written in the same six-line stanza form that Shakespeare used for *Venus and Adonis*. Originally, I planned to choose extracts, but the poem is so delightful that I could find almost nothing I wanted to cut. I decided to include the whole poem.

'The Church-Porch' is both a rhyming sermon and a seventeenth-century self-help manual, written in brilliantly epigrammatic verse. As I go about my daily life, phrases from this poem come into my mind remarkably often. 'Drink not the third glasse', for example, and, when I'm getting ready to go to church and can't find the right accessories, 'Stay not for th' other pin'. Others that float into consciousness on Sundays are: 'Judge not the preacher' and 'Jest not at preachers language, or expression'. When an editor asked me to contribute to a book the best piece of advice I'd ever been given, I sent Herbert's 'Dare to be true'.

The first of the poems from 'The Church', 'The Altar', is one of Herbert's pattern poems (often referred to nowadays as shape poems), in which the words are arranged into a recognizable shape. The form was not invented by Herbert but, when he had a go at it, the results were better than most. 'The Altar', and his other, and better, pattern poem, 'Easter-Wings', have become the best-known examples in the English language.

With 'Easter-Wings', a choice has to be made between printing the poem so that it looks like wings – in which case the reader has to turn the book sideways to read it – or printing it with the words the right way up. I have opted for the latter. In her book on Herbert, Julia Carolyn Guernsey points out that this way round it makes a picture of two hourglasses, another appropriate image.

Echo verse, too, was known before Herbert's time, but his

'Heaven' is arguably the best example in English. This beautiful poem, with its poignant questions and resonantly joyful conclusion, perfectly illustrates the coexistence in these poems of playfulness and seriousness.

Anyone who reads Herbert will be struck by the variety of forms he uses, and by his versatility and skill in finding appropriate forms for his subject matter. In 'A Wreath', he uses repetition so that the lines imitate their subject, overlapping, and coming full circle to where he began. In 'Sinnes Round', the repeated lines mimic what is happening in the poem, as they trap the speaker in a vicious circle. When he writes about Trinity Sunday, he does so in three tercets (three-line stanzas), and manages to work three sets of three ('heart, mouth, hands', etc.) into the last of them. In one of Herbert's most celebrated poems, 'The Collar', wildness and anger are reflected in the form of the poem, its irregular metre and rhyme scheme gradually settling down into a pattern towards the end.

Formal ingenuity is only one of the qualities that have made 'The Collar' a much praised and much anthologized poem. It is a good example of another of Herbert's strengths – his accuracy and honesty in describing his feelings and his spiritual experience. The speaker of the poem is disillusioned with the Christian life, feeling that all his sacrifices have brought him no rewards:

> Is the yeare onely lost to me?
> Have I no bayes to crown it?

He is ready to defy the fear of death and the afterlife and abandon his 'cage'.

> Away; take heed:
> I will abroad.
> Call in thy deaths head there...

In his booklet on Herbert's work, Kenneth Mason points out that this poem shows us we can be honest with God about our feelings, even when they are hostile. 'We *may* be angry, since he can take it.' God doesn't turn away from the furious Herbert, or punish him. He behaves like a mature adult dealing with an infantile tantrum.

> Me thoughts I heard one calling, *Child!*
> And I reply'd, *My Lord.*

Showing us that we needn't bottle up our feelings, says Mason, Herbert 'looks forward to modern psychology'. Dr Guernsey argues that the relationship between Herbert and his God is analogous to the relationship between the child and the 'good-enough' mother described in the work of the psychoanalyst Donald Winnicott. I have found this a helpful way of looking at the poems. The God who causes Herbert to grieve and complain when he seems absent (in 'The Search', for example) does, in other poems, resemble a good and loving parent. He is there when the child opens his eyes in the morning ('Mattens') and he puts us all safely to bed at night (Even-Song). In 'Whitsunday' he is 'The same sweet God of love and light', who can be trusted not to change. In 'Love', he is gentle, 'smiling', and reassuring, welcoming the soul to heaven.

'Love' is just one of the poems in which this often self-critical poet reminds himself, and his reader, that salvation depends, not on his merit, but on the love and grace of God. Sometimes the poems tread a complicated, tortuous path towards childlike acceptance of his love.

The greatest difficulty for a poet, says T. S. Eliot, is to distinguish between 'what one really feels and what one would like to feel'. I have been quoting these wise words for years. It is only while I've been working on this book that I discovered they come from an article on George Herbert. Eliot thought him 'as secure, as habitually sure as any poet who has written in English' at avoiding 'moments of falsity'.

Herbert himself says something similar to Eliot's dictum in one of my favourite poems, 'A True Hymne'. In the first stanza he complains that he can't think of anything to write except these words, *'My joy, my life, my crown'*. This is the second stanza:

> Yet slight not these few words:
> If truly said, they may take part
> Among the best in art.
> The finenesse which a hymne or psalme affords,
> Is, when the soul unto the lines accords.

And these lines are from the last stanza:

> Whereas if th' heart be moved,
> Although the verse be somewhat scant,
> God doth supplie the want.

Though he was capable of wonderful simplicity and directness, Herbert did not write poems that could ever be described as 'somewhat scant'. His work is rich with ingenious and beautiful images. There are extended metaphors, such as 'The Windows', where man is 'a brittle crazie glasse' through which 'light and glorie' may shine, and there are many felicitous moments like the well-observed 'But as birds drink, and straight lift up their head' ('Mans Medley').

And everywhere there are lines of breathtaking musicality:

> How fresh, O Lord, how sweet and clean
> Are thy returns! ev'n as the flowers in spring ('The Flower')

Softnesse, and peace, and joy, and love, and blisse ('Prayer').

It is sometimes possible for the reader to feel as Herbert did when he listened to church music:

> Now I in you without a bodie move,
> Rising and falling with your wings ('Church-Musick').

There are two poems I like because they reveal the humorous side of Herbert. One is 'Divinitie', where he pokes fun at those who enjoy the 'curious questions and divisions' of doctrinal argument. It is really quite simple, says Herbert.

> *Love God, and love your neighbour. Watch and pray.*
> *Do as ye would be done unto.*
> *O dark instructions; ev'n as dark as day!*
> *Who can these Gordian knots undo?*

In 'The Holy Communion (2)' (a poem not included in *The Temple*, and therefore kept separate here), he is witty and down-to-earth about the question of transubstantiation:

> *. . . whether bread stay*
> *Or whether Bread doe fly away*
> *Concerneth bread, not mee.*

In other words, it doesn't really matter all that much – an admirably broad-minded and Anglican view of the matter, or so it seems to me.

As an Anglican I can't help liking 'The British Church', though it isn't Herbert at his best, and 'To all Angels and Saints', where he explains why he does not 'addresse [his] vows' to the eponymous beings, or to the 'Mother of my God'.

In addition to the poems, I have included a chapter from Herbert's prose work *A Priest to the Temple* or *The Country Parson* (the latter was probably Herbert's own title). He wrote this at Bemerton. In a preface he explains that 'I have resolved to set down the Form and Character of a true Pastour, that I may hae a Mark to aim at'. I chose Chapter VI, 'The parson praying', because of some particularly enjoyable turns of phrase. The parson should speak slowly, he says, 'yet not so slow neither, as to let the fervency of the supplicant hang and dy between speaking'. And the congregation should make its responses 'not in a hudling, or slubbering fashion, gaping, or scratching the head, or spitting even in the midst of their answer'. That conjures up rather a vivid picture of behaviour in a seventeenth-century church service. Perhaps it isn't altogether surprising that the gentry, as we learn later in the chapter, often turned up halfway through.

The letter to Sir Henry Herbert is about their orphaned nieces, two of whom went to live with George and Jane at Bemerton. It shows Herbert as a concerned and considerate uncle, revealing that he insisted on taking care of 'both or neither' because one on her own might be lonely.

I have also made a selection from the 'Outlandish' (i.e. foreign) proverbs Herbert collected. Since he didn't actually write these, I was initially unsure about putting them in but David Scott, the editor of this series, urged me to do so, for the very good reason that they are fun. A few of Herbert's 1,032 proverbs are still current today, so I have included a couple that readers will be familiar with, but most of these were new to me.

My thanks to David for various pieces of good advice, to Lachlan Mackinnon for his invaluable help and support, and to Winchester College for allowing me to borrow a number of books on George Herbert from Moberly Library.

Wendy Cope
February 2002

# A Note on Reading Herbert

I have not modernized the spelling of the texts included here. This means that the reader can tell immediately when the participal ending '-ed' needs to be pronounced as a separate syllable. When written in full, it is sounded separately, so that, for example, 'borrowed' in Stanza One of 'The Pearl' is a three-syllable word rhyming with 'head'. The syllable is elided when the 'e' is replaced by an apostrophe ('blurr'd', 'call'd', 'shunn'd' in 'The Church-Porch').

Some other words need to be stressed in a way that is unfamiliar, if the line is to scan. In 'Sinnes Round' the stress falls on the first syllable of 'perfected'. And it is difficult to enjoy 'Heaven' without understanding that the stress falls on the second syllable of 'persever', making the closing rhyme a full one.

At the foot of each page there is a glossary of words likely to puzzle modern readers. In addition to these there are a few words that turn up repeatedly – I haven't glossed these every time. 'Then' often means 'than'. 'Still' can mean 'always'. 'Grief' often means physical as well as mental pain. 'Brave' can mean 'handsome and fully dressed'.

Some familiar words are spelled in an unfamiliar way. I have not glossed these, except where the spelling may cause misunderstanding (e.g. 'waving' for 'waiving' in 'The Dialogue'). I hope I am correct in assuming that spellings such as 'forrain', 'parrat' and 'dy' are not unrecognizable.

# The Dedication

Lord, my first fruits present themselves to thee;
Yet not mine neither: for from thee they came,
And must return. Accept of them and me,
And make us strive, who shall sing best thy name.
    Turn their eyes hither, who shall make a gain:
    Theirs, who shall hurt themselves or me, refrain.

# The Church-Porch

*Perirrhanterium*

1
Thou, whose sweet youth and early hopes inhance
Thy rate and price, and mark thee for a treasure;
Hearken unto a Verser, who may chance
Ryme thee to good, and make a bait of pleasure.
    A verse may finde him, who a sermon flies,
    And turn delight into a sacrifice.

2
Beware of lust: it doth pollute and foul
Whom God in Baptisme washt with his own blood.
It blots thy lesson written in thy soul;
The holy lines cannot be understood.
    How dare those eyes upon a Bible look,
    Much lesse towards God, whose lust is all their book?

3
Abstain wholly, or wed. Thy bounteous Lord
Allows thee choise of paths: take no by-wayes;
But gladly welcome what he doth afford;
Not grudging, that thy lust hath bounds and staies.
    Continence hath his joy: weigh both; and so
    If rottennesse have more, let Heaven go.

4
If God had laid all common, certainly
Man would have been th' incloser: but since now
God hath impal'd us, on the contrarie
Man breaks the fence, and every ground will plough.

*perirrhanterium*, an instrument for sprinkling holy water; *incloser*, one who appropriates common land to himself

O what were man, might he himself misplace!
Sure to be crosse he would shift feet and face.

5
Drink not the third glasse, which thou canst not tame,
When once it is within thee; but before
Mayst rule it, as thou list; and poure the shame,
Which it would poure on thee, upon the floore.
 It is most just to throw that on the ground,
 Which would throw me there, if I keep the round.

6
He that is drunken, may his mother kill
Bigge with his sister: he hath lost the reins,
Is outlawd by himself: all kinde of ill
Did with his liquour slide into his veins.
 The drunkard forfets Man, and doth devest
 All worldly right, save what he hath by beast.

7
Shall I, to please anothers wine-sprung minde,
Lose all mine own? God hath giv'n me a measure
Short of his canne and bodie; must I finde
A pain in that, wherein he findes a pleasure?
 Stay at the third glasse: if thou lose thy hold,
 Then thou art modest, and the wine grows bold.

8
If reason move not Gallants, quit the room,
(All in a shipwrack shift their severall way)
Let not a common ruine thee intombe:
Be not a beast in courtesie; but stay,
 Stay at the third cup, or forgo the place.
 Wine above all things doth Gods stamp deface.

### 9

Yet, if thou sinne in wine or wantonnesse,
Boast not thereof; nor make thy shame thy glorie.
Frailtie gets pardon by submissivenesse;
But he that boasts, shuts that out of his storie.
    He makes flat warre with God, and doth defie
    With his poore clod of earth the spacious sky.

### 10

Take not his name, who made thy mouth, in vain:
It gets thee nothing, and hath no excuse.
Lust and wine plead a pleasure, avarice gain:
But the cheap swearer through his open sluce
    Lets his soul runne for nought, as little fearing.
    Were I an *Epicure*, I could bate swearing.

### 11

When thou dost tell anothers jest, therein
Omit the oathes, which true wit cannot need:
Pick out of tales the mirth, but not the sinne.
He pares his apple, that will cleanly feed.
    Play not away the vertue of that name,
    Which is thy best stake, when griefs make thee tame.

### 12

The cheapest sinnes most dearely punisht are;
Because to shun them also is so cheap:
For we have wit to mark them, and to spare.
O crumble not away thy souls fair heap.
    If thou wilt die, the gates of hell are broad:
    Pride and full sinnes have made the way a road.

*bate*, give up

13
Lie not; but let thy heart be true to God,
Thy mouth to it, thy actions to them both:
Cowards tell lies, and those that fear the rod;
The stormie working soul spits lies and froth.
   Dare to be true. Nothing can need a ly:
   A fault, which needs it most, grows two thereby.

14
Flie idlenesse, which yet thou canst not flie
By dressing, mistressing, and complement.
If those take up thy day, the sunne will crie
Against thee: for his light was onely lent.
   God gave thy soul brave wings; put not those feathers
   Into a bed, to sleep out all ill weathers.

15
Art thou a Magistrate? then be severe:
If studious, copie fair, what time hath blurr'd;
Redeem truth from his jawes: if souldier,
Chase brave employments with a naked sword
   Throughout the world. Fool not: for all may have,
   If they dare try, a glorious life, or grave.

16
O England! full of sinne, but most of sloth;
Spit out thy flegme, and fill thy brest with glorie:
Thy Gentrie bleats, as if thy native cloth
Transfus'd a sheepishnesse into thy storie:
   Not that they all are so; but that the most
   Are gone to grasse, and in the pasture lost.

17
This losse springs chiefly from our education.
Some till their ground, but let weeds choke their sonne:
Some mark a partridge, never their childes fashion:

Some ship them over, and the thing is done.
    Studie this art, make it thy great designe;
    And if Gods image move thee not, let thine.

18
Some great estates provide, but doe not breed
A mast'ring minde; so both are lost thereby:
Or els they breed them tender, make them need
All that they leave: this is flat povertie.
    For he, that needs five thousand pound to live,
    Is full as poore as he, that needs but five.

19
The way to make thy sonne rich is to fill
His minde with rest, before his trunk with riches:
For wealth without contentment climbes a hill
To feel those tempests, which fly over ditches.
    But if thy sonne can make ten pound his measure,
    Then all thou addest may be call'd his treasure.

20
When thou dost purpose ought within thy power,
Be sure to doe it, though it be but small:
Constancie knits the bones, and makes us stowre,
When wanton pleasures becken us to thrall.
    Who breaks his own bond, forfeiteth himself:
    What nature made a ship, he makes a shelf.

21
Doe all things like a man, not sneakingly:
Think the king sees thee still; for his King does.
Simpring is but a lay-hypocrisie:
Give it a corner, and the clue undoes.
    Who fears to do ill, sets himself to task:
    Who fears to do well, sure should wear a mask.

*stowre*, sturdy

22
Look to thy mouth; diseases enter there.
Thou hast two sconses, if thy stomack call;
Carve, or discourse; do not a famine fear.
Who carves is kind to two; who talks, to all.
    Look on meat, think it dirt, then eat a bit;
    And say withall, Earth to earth I commit.

23
Slight those who say amidst their sickly healths,
Thou liv'st by rule. What doth not so, but man?
Houes are built by rule, and common-wealths.
Entice the trusty sunne, if that thou can,
    From his Ecliptick line: becken the skie.
    Who lives by rule then, keeps good companie.

24
Who keeps no guard upon himself, is slack,
And rots to nothing at the next great thaw.
Man is a shop of rules, a well truss'd pack,
Whose every parcell under-writes a law.
    Lose not thy self, nor give thy humours way:
    God gave them to thee under lock and key.

25
By all means use sometimes to be alone.
Salute thy self: see what thy soul doth wear.
Dare to look in thy chest, for 'tis thine own:
And tumble up and down what thou find'st there.
    Who cannot rest till hee good-fellows finde,
    He breaks up house, turns out of doores his minde.

*sconses*, safeguards; *under-writes*, subscribes to

26
Be thriftie, but not covetous: therefore give
Thy need, thine honour, and thy friend his due.
Never was scraper brave man. Get to live;
Then live, and use it: els, it is not true
    That thou hast gotten. Surely use alone
    Makes money not a contemptible stone.

27
Never exceed thy income. Youth may make
Ev'n with the yeare: but age, if it will hit,
Shoots a bow short, and lessens still his stake,
As the day lessens, and his life with it.
    Thy children, kindred, friends upon thee call;
    Before thy journey fairly part with all.

28
Yet in thy thriving still misdoubt some evil;
Lest gaining gain on thee, and make thee dimme
To all things els. Wealth is the conjurers devil;
Whom when he thinks he hath, the devil hath him.
    Gold thou mayst safely touch; but if it stick
    Unto thy hands, it woundeth to the quick.

29
What skills it, if a bag of stones or gold
About thy neck do drown thee? raise thy head;
Take starres for money; starres not to be told
By any art, yet to be purchased.
    None is so wastefull as the scraping dame.
    She loseth three for one; her soul, rest, fame.

*misdoubt*, suspect the existence of; *what skills it*, what difference does it make

30
By no means runne in debt: take thine own measure.
Who cannot live on twentie pound a yeare,
Cannot on fourtie: he's a man of pleasure,
A kinde of thing that's for it self too deere.
  The curious unthrift makes his clothes too wide,
  And spares himself, but would his taylor chide.

31
Spend not on hopes. They that by pleading clothes
Do fortunes seek, when worth and service fail,
Would have their tale beleeved for their oathes,
And are like empty vessels under sail.
  Old courtiers know this; therefore set out so,
  As all the day thou mayst hold out to go.

32
In clothes, cheap handsomnesse doth bear the bell.
Wisedome's a trimmer thing then shop e're gave.
Say not then, This with that lace will do well;
But, This with my discretion will be brave.
  Much curiousnesse is a perpetuall wooing,
  Nothing with labour, folly long a-doing.

33
Play not for gain, but sport. Who playes for more
Then he can lose with pleasure, stakes his heart;
Perhaps his wives too, and whom she hath bore:
Servants and churches also play their part.
  Onely a herauld, who that way doth passe,
  Findes his crackt name at length in the church-glasse.

*bear the bell*, win first prize

34
If yet thou love game at so deere a rate,
Learn this, that hath old gamesters deerely cost:
Dost lose? rise up: dost winne? rise in that state.
Who strive to sit out losing hands, are lost.
    Game is a civil gunpowder, in peace
    Blowing up houses with their whole increase.

35
In conversation boldnesse now bears sway.
But know, that nothing can so foolish be,
As empty boldnesse: therefore first assay
To stuffe thy minde with solid braverie;
    Then march on gallant: get substantiall worth.
    Boldnesse guilds finely, and will set it forth.

36
Be sweet to all. Is thy complexion sowre?
Then keep such companie; make them thy allay:
Get a sharp wife, a servant that will lowre.
A stumbler stumbles least in rugged way.
    Command thy self in chief. He lifes warre knows,
    Whom all his passions follow, as he goes.

37
Catch not at quarrels. He that dares not speak
Plainly and home, is coward of the two.
Think not thy fame at ev'ry twitch will break:
By great deeds shew, that thou canst little do;
    And do them not: that shall thy wisdome be;
    And change thy temperance into braverie.

*allay*, alloy

38
If that thy fame with ev'ry toy be pos'd,
'Tis a thinne webbe, which poysonous fancies make:
But the great souldiers honour was compos'd
Of thicker stuffe, which would endure a shake.
    Wisdome picks friends; civilitie playes the rest.
    A toy shunn'd cleanly passeth with the best.

39
Laugh not too much: the wittie man laughs least:
For wit is newes onely to ignorance.
Lesse at thine own things laugh; lest in the jest
Thy person share, and the conceit advance.
    Make not thy sport, abuses: for the fly
    That feeds on dung, is coloured thereby.

40
Pick out of mirth, like stones out of thy ground,
Profanenesse, filthinesse, abusivenesse.
These are the scumme, with which course wits abound:
The fine may spare these well, yet not go lesse.
    All things are bigge with jest: nothing that's plain,
    But may be wittie, if thou hast the vein.

41
Wit's an unruly engine, wildly striking
Sometimes a friend, sometimes the engineer.
Hast thou the knack? pamper it not with liking:
But if thou want it, buy it not too deere.
    Many, affecting wit beyond their power,
    Have got to be a deare fool for an houre.

*toy*, trifle

### 42

A sad wise valour is the brave complexion,
That leads the van, and swallows up the cities.
The gigler is a milk-maid, whom infection
Or a fir'd beacon frighteth from his ditties.
    Then he's the sport: the mirth then in him rests,
    And the sad man is cock of all his jests.

### 43

Towards great persons use respective boldnesse:
That temper gives them theirs, and yet doth take
Nothing from thine: in service, care or coldnesse
Doth ratably thy fortunes marre or make.
    Feed no man in his sinnes: for adulation
    Doth make thee parcell-devil in damnation.

### 44

Envie not greatnesse: for thou mak'st thereby
Thy self the worse, and so the distance greater.
Be not thine own worm: yet such jealousie,
As hurts not others, but may make thee better,
    Is a good spurre. Correct thy passions spite;
    Then may the beasts draw thee to happy light.

### 45

When basenesse is exalted, do not bate
The place its honour, for the persons sake.
The shrine is that which thou dost venerate,
And not the beast, that bears it on his back.
    I care not though the cloth of state should be
    Not of rich arras, but mean tapestrie.

*ratably*, proportionately; *parcell*, partly; *the beasts*, animal passions; *bate*, abate

46
Thy friend put in thy bosome: wear his eies
Still in thy heart, that he may see what's there.
If cause require, thou art his sacrifice;
Thy drops of bloud must pay down all his fear:
 But love is lost, the way of friendship's gone,
 Though *David* had his *Jonathan*, *Christ* his *John*.

47
Yet be not surety, if thou be a father.
Love is a personall debt. I cannot give
My childrens right, nor ought he take it: rather
Both friends should die, then hinder them to live.
 Fathers first enter bonds to natures ends;
 And are her sureties, ere they are a friends.

48
If thou be single, all thy goods and ground
Submit to love; but yet not more then all.
Give one estate, as one life. None is bound
To work for two, who brought himself to thrall.
 God made me one man; love makes me no more,
 Till labour come, and make my weaknesse score.

49
In thy discourse, if thou desire to please,
All such is courteous, usefull, new, or wittie.
Usefulnesse comes by labour, wit by ease;
Courtesie grows in court; news in the citie.
 Get a good stock of these, then draw the card
 That suites him best, of whom thy speech is heard.

50
Entice all neatly to what they know best;
For so thou dost thy self and him a pleasure:
(But a proud ignorance will lose his rest,

Rather then shew his cards.) Steal from his treasure
   What to ask further. Doubts well rais'd do lock
   The speaker to thee, and preserve thy stock.

51
If thou be Master-gunner, spend not all
That thou canst speak, at once; but husband it,
And give men turns of speech: do not forestall
By lavishnesse thine own, and others wit,
   As if thou mad'st thy will. A civil guest
   Will no more talk all, then eat all the feast.

52
Be calm in arguing: for fiercenesse makes
Errour a fault, and truth discourtesie.
Why should I feel another mans mistakes
More then his sicknesses or povertie?
   In love I should: but anger is not love,
   Nor wisdome neither: therefore gently move.

53
Calmnesse is great advantage: he that lets
Another chafe, may warm him at his fire,
Mark all his wandrings, and enjoy his frets;
As cunning fencers suffer heat to tire.
   Truth dwels not in the clouds: the bow that's there
   Doth often aim at, never hit the sphere.

54
Mark what another sayes: for many are
Full of themselves, and answer their own notion.
Take all into thee; then with equall care
Ballance each dramme of reason, like a potion.
   If truth be with thy friend, be with them both:
   Share in the conquest, and confesse a troth.

55
Be usefull where thou livest, that they may
Both want and wish thy pleasing presence still.
Kindnesse, good parts, great places are the way
To compasse this. Finde out mens wants and will,
   And meet them there. All worldly joyes go lesse
   To the one joy of doing kindnesses.

56
Pitch thy behaviour low, thy projects high;
So shalt thou humble and magnanimous be:
Sink not in spirit: who aimeth at the sky,
Shoots higher much then he that means a tree.
   A grain of glorie mixt with humblenesse
   Cures both a fever and lethargicknesse.

57
Let thy minde still be bent, still plotting where,
And when, and how the businesse may be done.
Slacknesse breeds worms; but the sure traveller,
Though he alight sometimes, still goeth on.
   Active and stirring spirits live alone.
   Write on the others, Here lies such a one.

58
Slight not the smallest losse, whether it be
In love or honour: take account of all;
Shine like the sunne in every corner: see
Whether thy stock of credit swell, or fall.
   Who say, I care not, those I give for lost;
   And to instruct them, will not quit the cost.

*quit*, repay

59
Scorn no mans love, though of a mean degree;
Love is a present for a mightie king.
Much lesse make any one thy enemie.
As gunnes destroy, so may a little sling.
    The cunning workman never doth refuse
    The meanest tool, that he may chance to use.

60
All forrain wisdome doth amount to this,
To take all that is given; whether wealth,
Or love, or language; nothing comes amisse:
A good digestion turneth all to health:
    And then as farre as fair behaviour may,
    Strike off all scores; none are so cleare as they.

61
Keep all thy native good, and naturalize
All forrain of that name; but scorn their ill:
Embrace their activenesse, not vanities.
Who follows all things, forfeiteth his will.
    If thou observest strangers in each fit,
    In time they'l runne thee out of all thy wit.

62
Affect in things about thee cleanlinesse,
That all may gladly board thee, as a flowre.
Slovens take up their stock of noisomnesse
Beforehand, and anticipate their last houre.
    Let thy mindes sweetnesse have his operation
    Upon thy body, clothes, and habitation.

*board*, approach

63
In Almes regard thy means, and others merit.
Think heav'n a better bargain, then to give
Onely thy single market-money for it.
Joyn hands with God to make a man to live.
    Give to all something; to a good poore man,
    Till thou change names, and be where he began.

64
Man is Gods image; but a poore man is
Christs stamp to boot: both images regard.
God reckons for him, counts the favour his:
Write, So much giv'n to God; thou shalt be heard.
    Let thy almes go before, and keep heav'ns gate
    Open for thee; or both may come too late.

65
Restore to God his due in tithe and time:
A tithe purloin'd cankers the whole estate.
Sundaies observe: think when the bells do chime,
'Tis angels musick; therefore come not late.
    God then deals blessings: If a king did so,
    Who would not haste, nay give, to see the show?

66
Twice on the day his due is understood;
For all the week thy food so oft he gave thee.
Thy cheere is mended; bate not of the food,
Because 'tis better, and perhaps may save thee.
    Thwart not the Mighty God: O be not crosse.
    Fast when thou wilt but then, 'tis gain not losse.

*single market-money*, small change

67
Though private prayer be a brave designe,
Yet publick hath more promises, more love:
And love's a weight to hearts, to eies a signe.
We all are but cold suitours; let us move
    Where it is warmest. Leave thy six and seven;
    Pray with the most: for where most pray, is heaven.

68
When once thy foot enters the church, be bare.
God is more there, then thou: for thou art there
Onely by his permission. Then beware,
And make thy self all reverence and fear.
    Kneeling ne're spoil'd silk stocking: quit thy state.
    All equal are within the churches gate.

69
Resort to sermons, but to prayers most:
Praying's the end of preaching. O be drest;
Stay not for th' other pin: why, thou hast lost
A joy for it worth worlds. Thus hell doth jest
    Away thy blessings, and extreamly flout thee,
    Thy clothes being fast, but thy soul loose about thee.

70
In time of service seal up both thine eies,
And send them to thine heart; that spying sinne,
They may weep out the stains by them did rise:
Those doores being shut, all by the eare comes in.
    Who marks in church-time others symmetrie,
    Makes all their beautie his deformitie.

*bare*, bare-headed

71
Let vain or busie thoughts have there no part:
Bring not thy plough, thy plots, thy pleasures thither.
Christ purg'd his temple; so must thou thy heart.
All worldly thoughts are but theeves met together
    To couzin thee. Look to thy actions well:
    For churches are either our heav'n or hell.

72
Judge not the preacher; for he is thy Judge:
If thou mislike him, thou conceiv'st him not.
God calleth preaching folly. Do not grudge
To pick out treasures from an earthen pot.
    The worst speak something good: if all want sense,
    God takes a text, and preacheth patience.

73
He that gets patience, and the blessing which
Preachers conclude with, hath not lost his pains.
He that by being at church escapes the ditch,
Which he might fall in by companions, gains.
    He that loves Gods abode, and to combine
    With saints on earth, shall one day with them shine.

74
Jest not at preachers language, or expression:
How know'st thou, but thy sinnes made him miscarrie?
Then turn thy faults and his into confession:
God sent him, whatsoe're he be: O tarry,
    And love him for his Master: his condition,
    Though it be ill, makes him no ill Physician.

75
None shall in hell such bitter pangs endure,
As those, who mock at Gods way of salvation.
Whom oil and balsames kill, what salve can cure?

They drink with greedinesse a full damnation.
    The Jews refused thunder; and we, folly.
    Though God do hedge us in, yet who is holy?

### 76

Summe up at night, what thou hast done by day;
And in the morning, what thou hast to do.
Dresse and undresse thy soul: mark the decay
And growth of it: if with thy watch, that too
    Be down, then winde up both; since we shall be
    Most surely judg'd, make thy accounts agree.

### 77

In brief, acquit thee bravely; play the man.
Look not on pleasures as they come, but go.
Deferre not the least vertue: lifes poore span
Make not an ell, by trifling in thy wo.
    If thou do ill; the joy fades, not the pains:
    If well; the pain doth fade, the joy remains.

*an ell*, 45 inches

## The Altar

A broken ALTAR, Lord, thy servant reares,
Made of a heart, and cemented with teares:
  Whose parts are as thy hand did frame;
  No workmans tool hath touch'd the same.
        A    HEART    alone
        Is   such   a   stone,
        As    nothing   but
        Thy pow'r doth cut.
        Wherefore each part
        Of my hard heart
        Meets in this frame,
        To praise thy name.
  That if I chance to hold my peace,
  These stones to praise thee may not cease.
O let thy blessed SACRIFICE be mine,
And sanctifie this ALTAR to be thine.

## The Reprisall

    I have consider'd it, and finde
There is no dealing with thy mighty passion:
For though I die for thee, I am behinde;
    My sinnes deserve the condemnation.

    O make me innocent, that I
May give a disentangled state and free:
And yet thy wounds still my attempts defie,
    For by thy death I die for thee.

    Ah! was it not enough that thou
By thy eternall glorie didst outgo me?
Couldst thou not griefs sad conquests me allow,
    But in all vict'ries overthrow me?

    Yet by confession will I come
Into thy conquest: though I can do nought
Against thee, in thee I will overcome
    The man, who once against thee fought.

## Redemption

Having been tenant long to a rich Lord,
    Not thriving, I resolved to be bold,
    And make a suit unto him, to afford
A new small-rented lease, and cancell th'old.
In heaven at his manour I him sought:
    They told me there, that he was lately gone
    About some land, which he had dearly bought
Long since on earth, to take possession.
I straight return'd, and knowing his great birth,
    Sought him accordingly in great resorts;
    In cities, theatres, gardens, parks, and courts:
At length I heard a ragged noise and mirth
    Of theeves and murderers: there I him espied,
    Who straight, *Your suit is granted*, said, & died.

## Easter

Rise heart; thy Lord is risen. Sing his praise
                Without delayes,
Who takes thee by the hand, that thou likewise
                With him mayst rise:
That, as his death calcined thee to dust,
His life may make thee gold, and much more, just.

Awake, my lute, and struggle for thy part
                With all thy art.
The crosse taught all wood to resound his name,
                Who bore the same.
His stretched sinews taught all strings, what key
Is best to celebrate this most high day.

Consort both heart and lute, and twist a song
                Pleasant and long:
Or, since all musick is but three parts vied
                And multiplied,
O let thy blessed Spirit bear a part,
And make up our defects with his sweet art.

    I got me flowers to straw thy way;
    I got me boughs off many a tree:
    But thou wast up by break of day,
    And brought'st thy sweets along with thee.

    The Sunne arising in the East,
    Though he give light, & th' East perfume;
    If they should offer to contest
    With thy arising, they presume.

    Can there be any day but this,
    Though many sunnes to shine endeavour?
    We count three hundred, but we misse:
    There is but one, and that one ever.

*calcined*, burned to ashes; *vied*, increased by addition or repetition

## Easter-Wings

Lord, who createdst man in wealth and store,
Though foolishly he lost the same,
Decaying more and more,
Till he became
Most poore:
With thee
O let me rise
As larks, harmoniously,
And sing this day thy victories:
Then shall the fall further the flight in me.

My tender age in sorrow did beginne:
And still with sicknesses and shame
Thou didst so punish sinne,
That I became
Most thinne.
With thee
Let me combine
And feel this day thy victorie:
For, if I imp my wing on thine,
Affliction shall advance the flight in me.

*imp*, in falconry 'to engraft feathers in a damaged wing, so as to restore or improve the powers of flight' (*OED*)

## Sinne

Lord, with what care hast thou begirt us round!
    Parents first season us: then schoolmasters
    Deliver us to laws; they send us bound
To rules of reason, holy messengers,
Pulpils and Sundayes, sorrow dogging sinne,
    Afflictions sorted, anguish of all sizes,
    Fine nets and stratagems to catch us in,
Bibles laid open, millions of surprises,
Blessings beforehand, tyes of gratefulness,
    The sound of glorie ringing in our eares:
    Without, our shame; within, our consciences;
Angels and grace, eternall hopes and fears.
    Yet all these fences and their whole aray
    One cunning bosome-sinne blows quite away.

## Affliction

When first thou didst entice to thee my heart,
                I thought the service brave:
So many joyes I writ down for my part,
                Besides what I might have
Out of my stock of naturall delights,
Augmented with thy gracious benefits.

I looked on thy furniture so fine,
                And made it fine to me:
Thy glorious houshold-stuffe did me entwine,
                And 'tice me unto thee.
Such starres I counted mine: both heav'n and earth
Payd me my wages in a world of mirth.

What pleasures could I want, whose King I served,
                Where joyes my fellows were?
Thus argu'd into hopes, my thoughts reserved
                No place for grief or fear.
Therefore my sudden soul caught at the place,
And made her youth and fiercenesse seek thy face.

At first thou gav'st me milk and sweetnesses;
                I had my wish and way:
My dayes were straw'd with flow'rs and happinesse;
                There was no moneth but May.
But with my yeares sorrow did twist and grow,
And made a partie unawares for wo.

My flesh began unto my soul in pain,
                Sicknesses cleave my bones;
Consuming agues dwell in ev'ry vein,
                And tune my breath to grones.
Sorrow was all my soul; I scarce beleeved,
Till grief did tell me roundly, that I lived.

When I got health, thou took'st away my life,
                    And more; for my friends die:
My mirth and edge was lost; a blunted knife
                    Was of more use then I.
Thus thinne and lean without a fence or friend,
I was blown through with ev'ry storm and winde.

Whereas my birth and spirit rather took
                    The way that takes the town;
Thou didst betray me to a lingring book,
                    And wrap me in a gown.
I was entangled in the world of strife,
Before I had the power to change my life.

Yet, for I threatned oft the siege to raise,
                    Not simpring all mine age,
Thou often didst with Academick praise
                    Melt and dissolve my rage.
I took thy sweetned pill, till I came where
I could not go away, nor persevere.

Yet lest perchance I should too happie be
                    In my unhappinesse,
Turning my purge to food, thou throwest me
                    Into more sicknesses.
Thus doth thy power crosse-bias me, not making
Thine own gift good, yet me from my wayes taking.

*crosse-bias*, deflect (as in bowls)

Now I am here, what thou wilt do with me
               None of my books will show:
I reade, and sigh, and wish I were a tree;
               For sure then I should grow
To fruit or shade: at least some bird would trust
Her houshold to me, and I should be just.

Yet, though thou troublest me, I must be meek;
               In weaknesse must be stout.
Well, I will change the service, and go seek
               Some other master out.
Ah my deare God! though I am clean forgot,
Let me not love thee, if I love thee not.

# Prayer

Prayer the Churches banquet, Angels age,
    Gods breath in man returning to his birth,
    The soul in paraphrase, heart in pilgrimage,
The Christian plummet sounding heav'n and earth;
Engine against th'Almightie, sinners towre,
    Reversed thunder, Christ-side-piercing spear,
    The six-daies world transposing in an houre,
A kind of tune, which all things heare and fear;
Softnesse, and peace, and joy, and love, and blisse,
    Exalted Manna, gladnesse of the best,
    Heaven in ordinarie, man well drest,
The milkie way, the bird of Paradise,
    Church-bels beyond the starres heard, the souls bloud,
    The land of spices; something understood.

## The Holy Communion (1)

Not in rich furniture, or fine aray,
      Nor in a wedge of gold,
      Thou, who for me wast sold,
   To me dost now thy self convey;
For so thou should'st without me still have been,
      Leaving within me sinne:

But by the way of nourishment and strength
      Thou creep'st into my breast;
      Making thy way my rest,
   And thy small quantities my length;
Which spread their forces into every part,
      Meeting sinnes force and art.

Yet can these not get over to my soul,
      Leaping the wall that parts
      Our souls and fleshy hearts;
   But as th' outworks, they may controll
My rebel-flesh, and carrying thy name,
      Affright both sinne and shame.

Onely thy grace, which with these elements comes,
      Knoweth the ready way,
      And hath the privie key,
   Op'ning the souls most subtile rooms;
While those to spirits refin'd, at doore attend
      Dispatches from their friend.

Give me my captive soul, or take
      My bodie also thither.
Another lift like this will make
      Them both to be together.

Before that sinne turn'd flesh to stone,
    And all our lump to leaven;
A fervent sigh might well have blown
    Our innocent earth to heaven.

For sure when Adam did not know
    To sinne, or sinne to smother;
He might to heav'n from Paradise go,
    As from one room t'another.

Thou hast restor'd us to this ease
    By this thy heav'nly bloud;
Which I can go to, when I please,
    And leave th' earth to their food.

# Antiphon

Cho.    Let all the world in ev'ry corner sing,
                    *My God and King.*

Vers.   The heav'ns are not too high,
        His praise may thither flie:
        The earth is not too low,
        His praises there may grow.

Cho.    Let all the world in ev'ry corner sing,
                    *My God and King.*

Vers.   The church with psalms must shout,
        No doore can keep them out:
        But above all, the heart
        Must bear the longest part.

Cho.    Let all the world in ev'ry corner sing,
                    *My God and King.*

# Employment

    If as a flowre doth spread and die,
      Thou wouldst extend me to some good,
  Before I were by frosts extremitie
                    Nipt in the bud;

    The sweetnesse and the praise were thine;
      But the extension and the room,
  Which in thy garland I should fill, were mine
                    At thy great doom.

    For as thou dost impart thy grace,
      The greater shall our glorie be.
  The measure of our joyes is in this place,
                    The stuffe with thee.

    Let me not languish then, and spend
      A life as barren to thy praise,
  As is the dust, to which that life doth tend,
                    But with delaies.

    All things are busie; onely I
      Neither bring hony with the bees,
  Nor flowres to make that, nor the husbandrie
                    To water these.

    I am no link of thy great chain,
      But all my companie is a weed.
  Lord place me in thy consort; give one strain
                    To my poore reed.

## The Holy Scriptures

Oh that I knew how all thy lights combine,
    And the configurations of their glorie!
    Seeing not onely how each verse doth shine,
But all the constellations of the storie.
This verse marks that, and both do make a motion
    Unto a third, that ten leaves off doth lie:
    Then as dispersed herbs do watch a potion,
These three make up some Christians destinie:
Such are thy secrets, which my life makes good,
    And comments on thee: for in ev'ry thing
    Thy words do finde me out, & parallels bring,
And in another make me understood.
    Starres are poore books, & oftentimes do misse:
    This book of starres lights to eternall blisse.

*watch a potion*, wait to be combined into a potion

## Whitsunday

    Listen sweet Dove unto my song,
    And spread thy golden wings in me;
    Hatching my tender heart so long,
Till it get wing, and flie away with thee.

    Where is that fire which once descended
    On thy Apostles? thou didst then
    Keep open house, richly attended,
Feasting all comers by twelve chosen men.

    Such glorious gifts thou didst bestow,
    That th' earth did like a heav'n appeare;
    The starres were coming down to know
If they might mend their wages, and serve here.

    The sunne, which once did shine alone,
    Hung down his head, and wisht for night,
    When he beheld twelve sunnes for one
Going about the world, and giving light.

    But since those pipes of gold, which brought
    That cordiall water to our ground,
    Were cut and martyr'd by the fault
Of those, who did themselves through their side wound,

    Thou shutt'st the doore, and keep'st within;
    Scarce a good joy creeps through the chink:
    And if the braves of conqu'ring sinne
Did not excite thee, we should wholly sink.

    Lord, though we change, thou art the same;
    The same sweet God of love and light:
    Restore this day, for thy great name,
Unto his ancient and miraculous right.

## Mattens

    I cannot ope mine eyes,
  But thou art ready there to catch
  My morning-soul and sacrifice:
Then we must needs for that day make a match.

    My God, what is a heart?
  Silver, or gold, or precious stone,
  Or starre, or rainbow, or a part
Of all these things, or all of them in one?

    My God, what is a heart,
  That thou shouldst it so eye, and wooe,
  Powring upon it all thy art,
As if that thou hadst nothing els to do?

    Indeed mans whole estate
  Amounts (and richly) to serve thee:
  He did not heav'n and earth create,
Yet studies them, not him by whom they be.

    Teach me thy love to know;
  That this new light, which now I see,
  May both the work and workman show:
Then by a sunne-beam I will climbe to thee.

## Even-Song

Blest be the God of love,
Who gave me eyes, and light, and power this day,
Both to be busie, and to play.
But much more blest be God above,
Who gave me sight alone,
Which to himself he did denie:
For when he sees my waies, I dy:
But I have got his sonne, and he hath none.

What have I brought thee home
For this thy love? have I discharg'd the debt,
Which this dayes favour did beget?
I ranne; but all I brought, was fome.
Thy diet, care, and cost
Do end in bubbles, balls of winde;
Of winde to thee whom I have crost,
But balls of wilde-fire to my troubled minde.

Yet still thou goest on,
And now with darknesse closest wearie eyes,
Saying to man, *It doth suffice:*
*Henceforth repose; your work is done.*
Thus in thy ebony box
Thou dost inclose us, till the day
Put our amendment in our way,
And give new wheels to our disorder'd clocks.

I muse, which shows more love,
The day or night: that is the gale, this th' harbour;
That is the walk, and this the arbour;
Or that the garden, this the grove.
My God, thou art all love.
Not one poore minute scapes thy breast,
But brings a favour from above;
And in this love, more then in bed, I rest.

## Church-Musick

Sweetest of sweets, I thank you: when displeasure
        Did through my bodie wound my minde,
You took me thence, and in your house of pleasure
        A daintie lodging me assign'd.

Now I in you without a bodie move,
        Rising and falling with your wings:
We both together sweetly live and love,
        Yet say sometimes, *God help poore Kings.*

Comfort, I'le die; for if you poste from me,
        Sure I shall do so, and much more:
But if I travell in your companie,
        You know the way to heavens doore.

## The Windows

Lord, how can man preach thy eternall word?
      He is a brittle crazie glasse:
Yet in thy temple thou dost him afford
          This glorious and transcendent place,
      To be a window, through thy grace.

But when thou dost anneal in glasse thy storie,
      Making thy life to shine within
The holy Preachers; then the light and glorie
          More rev'rend grows, & more doth win:
      Which else shows watrish, bleak, & thin.

Doctrine and life, colours and light, in one
      When they combine and mingle, bring
A strong regard and aw: but speech alone
          Doth vanish like a flaring thing,
      And in the eare, not conscience ring.

*anneal*, burn in colours upon glass

## Trinitie Sunday

Lord, who hast form'd me out of mud,
    And hast redeem'd me through thy bloud,
    And sanctifi'd me to do good;

Purge all my sinnes done heretofore:
    For I confesse my heavie score,
    And I will strive to sinne no more.

Enrich my heart, mouth, hands in me,
    With faith, with hope, with charitie;
    That I may runne, rise, rest with thee.

# Content

Peace mutt'ring thoughts, and do not grudge to keep
        Within the walls of your own breast:
Who cannot on his own bed sweetly sleep,
        Can on anothers hardly rest.

Gad not abroad at ev'ry quest and call
        Of an untrained hope or passion.
To court each place or fortune that doth fall,
        Is wantonnesse in contemplation.

Mark how the fire in flints doth quiet lie,
        Content and warm t' it self alone:
But when it would appear to others eye,
        Without a knock it never shone.

Give me the pliant minde, whose gentle measure
        Complies and suits with all estates;
Which can let loose to a crown, and yet with pleasure
        Take up within a cloisters gates.

This soul doth span the world, and hang content
        From either pole unto the centre:
Where in each room of the well-furnisht tent
        He lies warm, and without adventure.

The brags of life are but a nine dayes wonder;
        And after death the fumes that spring
From private bodies make as big a thunder,
        As those which rise from a huge King.

Onely thy Chronicle is lost; and yet
        Better by worms be all once spent,
Then to have hellish moths still gnaw and fret
        Thy name in books, which may not rent:

*let loose to*, aim at

When all thy deeds, whose brunt thou feel'st alone,
      Are chaw'd by others pens and tongue;
And as their wit is, their digestion,
      Thy nourisht fame is weak or strong.

Then cease discoursing soul, till thine own ground,
      Do not thy self or friends importune.
He that by seeking hath himseif once found,
      Hath ever found a happie fortune.

## The Quidditie

My God, a verse is not a crown,
No point of honour, or gay suit,
No hawk, or banquet, or renown,
Nor a good sword, nor yet a lute:

It cannot vault, or dance, or play;
It never was in *France* or *Spain*;
Nor can it entertain the day
With my great stable or demain:

It is no office, art, or news,
Nor the Exchange, or busie Hall;
But it is that which while I use
I am with thee, and *most take all*.

## Avarice

Money, thou bane of blisse, & sourse of wo,
        Whence com'st thou, that thou art so fresh and fine?
        I know thy parentage is base and low:
Man found thee poore and dirtie in a mine.
Surely thou didst so little contribute
        To this great kingdome, which thou now hast got,
        That he was fain, when thou wert destitute,
To digge thee out of thy dark cave and grot:
Then forcing thee by fire he made thee bright:
        Nay, thou hast got the face of man; for we
        Have with our stamp and seal transferr'd our right:
Thou art the man, and man but drosse to thee.
        Man calleth thee his wealth, who made thee rich;
        And while he digs out thee, falls in the ditch.

## To all Angels and Saints

Oh glorious spirits, who after all your bands
See the smooth face of God without a frown
                Or strict commands;
Where ev'ry one is king, and hath his crown,
If not upon his head, yet in his hands:

Not out of envie or maliciousnesse
Do I forbear to crave your speciall aid:
                I would addresse
My vows to thee most gladly, Blessed Maid,
And Mother of my God, in my distresse.

Thou art the holy mine, whence came the gold,
The great restorative for all decay
                In young and old;
Thou art the cabinet where the jewell lay:
Chiefly to thee would I my soul unfold:

But now, alas, I dare not; for our King,
Whom we do all joyntly adore and praise,
                Bids no such thing:
And where his pleasure no injunction layes,
('Tis your own case) ye never move a wing.

All worship is prerogative, and a flower
Of his rich crown, from whom lyes no appeal
                At the last houre:
Therefore we dare not from his garland steal,
To make a posie for inferiour power.

Although then others court you, if ye know
What's done on earth, we shall not fare the worse,
                Who do not so;
Since we are ever ready to disburse,
If any one our Masters hand can show.

*after all your bands,* freed from your bonds or according to your ranks

# Deniall

When my devotions could not pierce
        Thy silent eares;
Then was my heart broken, as was my verse:
        My breast was full of fears
           And disorder:

My bent thoughts, like a brittle bow,
        Did flie asunder:
Each took his way; some would to pleasures go,
        Some to the warres and thunder
           Of alarms.

As good go any where, they say,
        As to benumme
Both knees and heart, in crying night and day,
        *Come, come, my God, O come,*
           But no hearing.

O that thou shouldst give dust a tongue
        To crie to thee,
And then not heare it crying! all day long
        My heart was in my knee,
           But no hearing.

Therefore my soul lay out of sight,
        Untun'd, unstrung:
My feeble spirit, unable to look right,
        Like a nipt blossome, hung
           Discontented.

O cheer and tune my heartlesse breast,
        Deferre no time;
That so thy favours granting my request,
        They and my minde may chime,
           And mend my ryme.

## Vertue

Sweet day, so cool, so calm, so bright,
The bridall of the earth and skie:
The dew shall weep thy fall to night;
                For thou must die.

Sweet rose, whose hue angrie and brave
Bids the rash gazer wipe his eye:
Thy root is ever in its grave,
                And thou must die.

Sweet spring, full of sweet dayes and roses,
A box where sweets compacted lie;
My musick shows ye have your closes,
                And all must die.

Onely a sweet and vertuous soul,
Like season'd timber, never gives;
But though the whole world turn to coal,
                Then chiefly lives.

## The Pearl

I know the wayes of Learning; both the head
And pipes that feed the presse, and make it runne;
What reason hath from nature borrowed,
Or of it self, like a good huswife, spunne
In laws and policie; what the starres conspire,
What willing nature speaks, what forc'd by fire;
Both th' old discoveries, and the new-found seas,
The stock and surplus, cause and historie:
All these stand open, or I have the keyes:
                  Yet I love thee.

I know the wayes of Honour, what maintains
The quick returns of courtesie and wit:
In vies of favours whether partie gains;
When glorie swells the heart, and moldeth it
To all expressions both of hand and eye,
Which on the world a true-love-knot may tie,
And bear the bundle, wheresoe're it goes:
How many drammes of spirit there must be
To sell my life unto my friends or foes:
                  Yet I love thee.

I know the wayes of Pleasure, the sweet strains,
The lullings and the relishes of it;
The propositions of hot bloud and brains;
What mirth and musick mean; what love and wit
Have done these twentie hundred yeares, and more:
I know the projects of unbridled store:
My stuffe is flesh, not brasse; my senses live,
And grumble oft, that they have more in me
Then he that curbs them, being but one to five:
                  Yet I love thee.

I know all these, and have them in my hand:
Therefore not sealed, but with open eyes
I flie to thee, and fully understand
Both the main sale, and the commodities;
And at what rate and price I have thy love;
With all the circumstances that may move:
Yet through these labyrinths, not my groveling wit,
But thy silk twist let down from heav'n to me,
Did both conduct and teach me, how by it
      To climbe to thee.

## Unkindnesse

Lord, make me coy and tender to offend:
In friendship, first I think, if that agree,
    Which I intend,
  Unto my friends intent and end.
I would not use a friend, as I use Thee.

If any touch my friend, or his good name,
It is my honour and my love to free
    His blasted fame
  From the least or thought of blame.
I could not use a friend, as I use Thee.

My friend may spit upon my curious floore:
Would he have gold? I lend it instantly;
    But let the poore,
  And thou within them, starve at doore.
I cannot use a friend, as I use Thee.

When that my friend pretendeth to a place,
I quit my interest, and leave it free:
    But when thy grace
  Sues for my heart, I thee displace,
Nor would I use a friend, as I use Thee.

Yet can a friend what thou hast done fulfill?
O write in brasse, *My God upon a tree*
    *His bloud did spill*
  *Onely to purchase my good-will.*
Yet use I not my foes, as I use Thee.

# Life

I made a posie, while the day ran by:
Here will I smell my remnant out, and tie
                My life within this band.
But Time did becken to the flowers, and they
By noon most cunningly did steal away,
                And wither'd in my hand.

My hand was next to them, and then my heart:
I took, without more thinking, in good part
                Times gentle admonition:
Who did so sweetly deaths sad taste convey,
Making my minde to smell my fatall day;
                Yet sugring the suspicion.

Farewell deare flowers, sweetly your time ye spent,
Fit, while ye liv'd, for smell or ornament,
                And after death for cures.
I follow straight without complaints or grief,
Since if my sent be good, I care not if
                It be as short as yours.

## Mortification

How soon doth man decay!
When clothes are taken from a chest of sweets
    To swaddle infants, whose young breath
        Scarce knows the way;
    Those clouts are little winding sheets,
Which do consigne and send them unto death.

    When boyes go first to bed,
They step into their voluntarie graves,
    Sleep bindes them fast; onely their breath
        Makes them not dead:
    Successive nights, like rolling waves,
Convey them quickly, who are bound for death.

    When youth is frank and free,
And calls for musick, while his veins do swell,
    All day exchanging mirth and breath
        In companie;
    That musick summons to the knell,
Which shall befriend him at the houre of death.

    When man grows staid and wise,
Getting a house and home, where he may move
    Within the circle of his breath,
        Schooling his eyes;
    That dumbe inclosure maketh love
Unto the coffin, that attends his death.

    When age grows low and weak,
Marking his grave, and thawing ev'ry yeare,
    Till all do melt, and drown his breath
        When he would speak;
    A chair or litter shows the biere,
Which shall convey him to the house of death.

    Man, ere he is aware,

> Hath put together a solemnitie,
>    And drest his herse, while he has breath
>       As yet to spare:
>    Yet Lord, instruct us so to die,
> That all these dyings may be life in death.

## Jordan

When first my lines of heav'nly joyes made mention,
Such was their lustre, they did so excell,
That I sought out quaint words, and trim invention;
My thoughts began to burnish, sprout, and swell,
Curling with metaphors a plain intention,
Decking the sense, as if it were to sell.

Thousands of notions in my brain did runne,
Off'ring their service, if I were not sped:
I often blotted what I had begunne;
This was not quick enough, and that was dead.
Nothing could seem too rich to clothe the sunne,
Much lesse those joyes which trample on his head.

As flames do work and winde, when they ascend,
So did I weave my self into the sense.
But while I bustled, I might heare a friend
Whisper, *How wide is all this long pretence!*
*There is in love a sweetnesse readie penn'd:*
*Copie out onely that, and save expense.*

## Conscience

      Peace pratler, do not lowre:
Not a fair look, but thou dost call it foul:
Not a sweet dish, but thou dost call it sowre:
        Musick to thee doth howl.
    By listning to thy chatting fears
    I have both lost mine eyes and eares.

      Pratler, no more, I say:
My thoughts must work, but like a noiselesse sphere;
Harmonious peace must rock them all the day:
        No room for pratlers there.
    If thou persistest, I will tell thee,
    That I have physick to expell thee.

      And the receit shall be
My Saviours bloud: when ever at his board
I do but taste it, straight it cleanseth me,
        And leaves thee not a word;
    No, not a tooth or nail to scratch,
    And at my actions carp, or catch.

      Yet if thou talkest still,
Besides my physick, know there's some for thee:
Some wood and nails to make a staffe or bill
        For those that trouble me:
    The bloudie crosse of my deare Lord
    Is both my physick and my sword.

*receit*, formula for prescription

## The British Church

I joy, deare Mother, when I view
Thy perfect lineaments and hue
      Both sweet and bright.
Beautie in thee takes up her place,
And dates her letters from thy face,
      When she doth write.

A fine aspect in fit aray,
Neither too mean, nor yet too gay,
      Shows who is best.
Outlandish looks may not compare:
For all they either painted are,
      Or else undrest.

She on the hills, which wantonly
Allureth all in hope to be
      By her preferr'd,
Hath kiss'd so long her painted shrines,
That ev'n her face by kissing shines,
      For her reward.

She in the valley is so shie
Of dressing, that her hair doth lie
      About her eares:
While she avoids her neighbours pride,
She wholly goes on th' other side,
      And nothing wears.

But, dearest Mother, what those misse,
The mean, thy praise and glorie is,
      And long may be.
Blessed be God, whose love it was
To double-moat thee with his grace,
      And none but thee.

*outlandish*, foreign

# The Quip

The merrie world did on a day
With his train-bands and mates agree
To meet together, where I lay,
And all in sport to geere at me.

First, Beautie crept into a rose,
Which when I pluckt not, Sir, said she,
Tell me, I pray, Whose hands are those?
*But thou shalt answer, Lord, for me.*

Then Money came, and chinking still,
What tune is this, poore man? said he:
I heard in Musick you had skill.
*But thou shalt answer, Lord, for me.*

Then came brave Glorie puffing by
In silks that whistled, who but he?
He scarce allow'd me half an eie.
*But thou shalt answer, Lord, for me.*

Then came quick Wit and Conversation,
And he would needs a comfort be,
And, to be short, make an Oration.
*But thou shalt answer, Lord, for me.*

Yet when the houre of thy designe
To answer these fine things shall come;
Speak not at large; say, I am thine:
And then they have their answer home.

---

*train-bands*, trained bands of citizen soldiers; *geerse*, jeer

## Dialogue

Sweetest Saviour, if my soul
      Were but worth the having,
Quickly should I then controll
      Any thought of waving.
But when all my care and pains
Cannot give the name of gains
To thy wretch so full of stains,
What delight or hope remains?

*What, Child, is the ballance thine,*
      *Thine the poise and measure?*
*If I say, Thou shalt be mine;*
      *Finger not my treasure.*
*What the gains in having thee*
*Do amount to, onely he,*
*Who for man was sold, can see;*
*That transferr'd th' accounts to me.*

But as I can see no merit,
      Leading to this favour:
So the way to fit me for it
      Is beyond my savour.
As the reason then is thine;
So the way is none of mine:
I disclaim the whole designe:
Sinne disclaims and I resigne.

*That is all, if that I could*
      *Get without repining;*
*And my clay, my creature, would*
      *Follow my resigning:*
*That as I did freely part*
*With my glorie and desert,*
*Left all joyes to feel all smart* –
      Ah! no more: thou break'st my heart.

*waving,* waiving; *savour,* perception, understanding

# Providence

O sacred Providence, who from end to end
Strongly and sweetly movest, shall I write,
And not of thee, through whom my fingers bend
To hold my quill? shall they not do thee right?

Of all the creatures both in sea and land
Onely to Man thou hast made known thy wayes,
And put the penne alone into his hand,
And made him Secretarie of thy praise.

Beasts fain would sing; birds dittie to their notes;
Trees would be tuning on their native lute
To thy renown: but all their hands and throats
Are brought to Man, while they are lame and mute.

Man is the worlds high Priest: he doth present
The sacrifice for all; while they below
Unto the service mutter an assent,
Such as springs use that fall, and windes that blow.

He that to praise and laud thee doth refrain,
Doth not refrain unto himself alone,
But robs a thousand who would praise thee fain,
And doth commit a world of sinne in one.

The beasts say, Eat me: but, if beasts must teach,
The tongue is yours to eat, but mine to praise.
The trees say, Pull me: but the hand you stretch,
Is mine to write, as it is yours to raise.

Wherefore, most sacred Spirit, I here present
For me and all my fellows praise to thee:
And just it is that I should pay the rent,
Because the benefit accrues to me.

We all acknowledge both thy power and love
To be exact, transcendent, and divine;
Who dost so strongly and so sweetly move,
While all things have their will, yet none but thine.

For either thy command or thy permission
Lay hands on all: they are thy right and left.
The first puts on with speed and expedition;
The other curbs sinnes stealing pace and theft.

Nothing escapes them both; all must appeare,
And be dispos'd, and dress'd, and tun'd by thee,
Who sweetly temper'st all. If we could heare
Thy skill and art, what musick would it be!

Thou art in small things great, not small in any:
Thy even praise can neither rise, nor fall.
Thou art in all things one, in each thing many:
For thou art infinite in one and all.

Tempests are calm to thee; they know thy hand,
And hold it fast, as children do their fathers,
Which crie and follow. Thou hast made poore sand
Check the proud sea, ev'n when it swells and gathers.

Thy cupboard serves the world: the meat is set,
Where all may reach: no beast but knows his feed.
Birds teach us hawking; fishes have their net:
The great prey on the lesse, they on some weed.

Nothing ingendred doth prevent his meat:
Flies have their table spread, ere they appeare.
Some creatures have in winter what to eat;
Others do sleep, and envie not their cheer.

*prevent*, precede

How finely dost thou times and seasons spin,
And make a twist checker'd with night and day!
Which as it lengthens windes, and windes us in,
As bouls go on, but turning all the way.

Each creature hath a wisdome for his good.
The pigeons feed their tender off-spring, crying,
When they are callow; but withdraw their food
When they are fledge, that need may teach them flying.

Bees work for man; and yet they never bruise
Their masters flower, but leave it, having done,
As fair as ever, and as fit to use;
So both the flower doth stay, and hony run.

Sheep eat the grasse, and dung the ground for more:
Trees after bearing drop their leaves for soil:
Springs vent their streams, and by expense get store:
Clouds cool by heat, and baths by cooling boil.

Who hath the vertue to expresse the rare
And curious vertues both of herbs and stones?
Is there an herb for that? O that thy care
Would show a root, that gives expressions!

And if an herb hath power, what have the starres?
A rose, besides his beautie, is a cure.
Doubtlesse our plagues and plentie, peace and warres
Are there much surer then our art is sure.

Thou hast hid metals: man may take them thence;
But at his perill: when he digs the place,
He makes a grave; as if the thing had sense,
And threatned man, that he should fill the space.

*boul*, bowl

Ev'n poysons praise thee. Should a thing be lost?
Should creatures want for want of heed their due?
Since where are poysons, antidotes are most:
The help stands close, and keeps the fear in view.

The sea, which seems to stop the traveller,
Is by a ship the speedier passage made.
The windes, who think they rule the mariner,
 Are rul'd by him, and taught to serve his trade.

And as thy house is full, so I adore
Thy curious art in marshalling thy goods.
The hills with health abound; the vales with store;
The South with marble; North with furres & woods.

Hard things are glorious: easie things good cheap.
The common all men have; that which is rare
Men therefore seek to have, and care to keep.
The healthy frosts with summer-fruits compare.

Light without winde is glasse: warm without weight
Is wooll and furre: cool without closenesse, shade:
Speed without pains, a horse: tall without height,
A servile hawk: low without losse, a spade.

All countreys have enough to serve their need:
If they seek fine things, thou dost make them run
For their offence; and then dost turn their speed
To be commerce and trade from sunne to sunne.

Nothing wears clothes, but Man; nothing doth need
But he to wear them. Nothing useth fire,
But Man alone, to show his heav'nly breed:
And onely he hath fuell in desire.

When th' earth was dry, thou mad'st a sea of wet:
When that lay gather'd, thou didst broach the mountains:
When yet some places could no moisture get,
The windes grew gard'ners, and the clouds good fountains.

Rain, do not hurt my flowers; but gently spend
Your hony drops: presse not to smell them here:
When they are ripe, their odour will ascend,
And at your lodging with their thanks appeare.

How harsh are thorns to pears! and yet they make
A better hedge, and need lesse reparation.
How smooth are silks compared with a stake,
Or with a stone! yet make no good foundation.

Sometimes thou dost divide thy gifts to man,
Sometimes unite. The Indian nut alone
Is clothing, meat and trencher, drink and can,
Boat, cable, sail and needle, all in one.

Most herbs that grow in brooks, are hot and dry.
Cold fruits warm kernells help against the winde.
The lemmons juice and rinde cure mutually.
The whey of milk doth loose, the milk doth binde.

Thy creatures leap not, but expresse a feast,
Where all the guests sit close, and nothing wants.
Frogs marry fish and flesh; bats, bird and beast;
Sponges, non-sense and sense; mines, th' earth & plants.

To show thou art not bound, as if thy lot
Were worse then ours, sometimes thou shiftest hands.
Most things move th' under-jaw; the Crocodile not.
Most things sleep lying; th' Elephant leans or stands.

*Indian nut*, coconut; *marry*, combine

But who hath praise enough? nay, who hath any?
None can expresse thy works, but he that knows them:
And none can know thy works, which are so many,
And so complete, but onely he that owes them.

All things that are, though they have sev'rall wayes,
Yet in their being joyn with one advise
To honour thee: and so I give thee praise
In all my other hymnes, but in this twice.

Each thing that is, although in use and name
It go for one, hath many wayes in store
To honour thee; and so each hymne thy fame
Extolleth many wayes, yet this one more.

## Sinnes Round

Sorrie I am, my God, sorrie I am,
That my offences course it in a ring.
My thoughts are working like a busie flame,
Untill their cockatrice they hatch and bring:
And when they once have perfected their draughts,
My words take fire from my inflamed thoughts.

My words take fire from my inflamed thoughts,
Which spit it forth like the Sicilian Hill.
They vent the wares, and passe them with their faults,
And by their breathing ventilate the ill.
But words suffice not, where are lewd intentions:
My hands do joyn to finish the inventions.

My hands do joyn to finish the inventions:
And so my sinnes ascend three stories high,
As Babel grew, before there were dissensions.
Yet ill deeds loyter not: for they supplie
New thoughts of sinning: wherefore, to my shame,
Sorrie I am, my God, sorrie I am.

*cockatrice*, serpent fabled to kill by its glance, and to be hatched from a cock's egg

## Peace

Sweet Peace, where dost thou dwell? I humbly crave,
              Let me once know.
  I sought thee in a secret cave,
            And ask'd, if Peace were there.
A hollow winde did seem to answer, No:
              Go seek elsewhere.

I did; and going did a rainbow note:
              Surely, thought I,
  This is the lace of Peaces coat:
            I will search out the matter.
But while I lookt, the clouds immediately
              Did break and scatter.

Then went I to a garden, and did spy
              A gallant flower,
  The Crown Imperiall: Sure, said I,
            Peace at the root must dwell.
But when I digg'd, I saw a worm devoure
              What show'd so well.

At length I met a rev'rend good old man,
            Whom when for Peace
  I did demand, he thus began:
            There was a Prince of old
At Salem dwelt, who liv'd with good increase
              Of flock and fold.

He sweetly liv'd; yet sweetnesse did not save
              His life from foes.
  But after death out of his grave
            There sprang twelve stalks of wheat:
Which many wondring at, got some of those
            To plant and set.

It prosper'd strangely, and did soon disperse
                Through all the earth:
For they that taste it do rehearse,
          That vertue lies therein,
A secret vertue bringing peace and mirth
                By flight of sinne.

Take of this grain, which in my garden grows,
                And grows for you;
Make bread of it: and that repose
            And peace, which ev'ry where
With so much earnestnesse you do pursue,
                Is onely there.

## Mans Medley

Heark, how the birds do sing,
        And woods do ring.
All creatures have their joy: and man hath his.
        Yet if we rightly measure,
                Mans joy and pleasure
Rather hereafter, then in present, is.

        To this life things of sense
                Make their pretence:
In th' other Angels have a right by birth:
        Man ties them both alone,
                And makes them one,
With th' one hand touching heav'n, with th' other earth.

        In soul he mounts and flies,
                In flesh he dies.
He wears a stuffe whose thread is course and round,
        But trimm'd with curious lace,
                And should take place
After the trimming, not the stuffe and ground.

        Not that he may not here
                Taste of the cheer,
But as birds drink, and straight lift up their head,
        So he must sip and think
                Of better drink
He may attain to, after he is dead.

---

*medley*, 'a cloth woven with wools of different colours or shades' (*OED*), as well as a musical composition.

>             But as his joyes are double;
>                 So is his trouble.
>     He hath two winters, other things but one:
>             Both frosts and thoughts do nip,
>                 And bite his lip;
>     And he of all things fears two deaths alone.
>
>             Yet ev'n the greatest griefs
>                 May be reliefs,
>     Could he but take them right, and in their wayes.
>             Happie is he, whose heart
>                 Hath found the art
>     To turn his double pains to double praise.

## The Storm

If as the windes and waters here below
                  Do flie and flow,
My sighs and tears as busie were above;
                  Sure they would move
And much affect thee, as tempestuous times
Amaze poore mortals, and object their crimes.

Starres have their storms, ev'n in a high degree,
                  As well as we.
A throbbing conscience spurred by remorse
                  Hath a strange force:
It quits the earth, and mounting more and more
Dares to assault thee, and besiege thy doore.

There it stands knocking, to thy musicks wrong,
                  And drowns the song.
Glorie and honour are set by, till it
                  An answer get.
Poets have wrong'd poore storms: such dayes are best;
They purge the aire without, within the breast.

*object*, express disapproval of

# The Method

    Poore heart, lament.
For since thy God refuseth still,
There is some rub, some discontent,
    Which cools his will.

    Thy Father could
Quickly effect, what thou dost move;
For he is *Power*: and sure he would;
    For he is *Love*.

    Go search this thing,
Tumble thy breast, and turn thy book.
If thou hadst lost a glove or ring,
    Wouldst thou not look?

    What do I see
Written above there? *Yesterday*
*I did behave me carelesly,*
    *When I did pray.*

    And should Gods eare
To such indifferents chained be,
Who do not their own motions heare?
    Is God lesse free?

    But stay! what's there?
*Late when I would have something done,*
*I had a motion to forbear,*
    *Yet I went on.*

    And should Gods eare,
Which needs not man, be ty'd to those
Who heare not him, but quickly heare
    His utter foes?

Then once more pray:
Down with thy knees, up with thy voice.
Seek pardon first, and God will say,
*Glad heart rejoyce.*

## Divinitie

As men, for fear the starres should sleep and nod,
    And trip at night, have spheres suppli'd;
As if a starre were duller then a clod,
    Which knows his way without a guide:

Just so the other heav'n they also serve,
    Divinities transcendent skie:
Which with the edge of wit they cut and carve.
    Reason triumphs, and faith lies by.

Could not that Wisdome, which first broacht the wine,
    Have thicken'd it with definitions?
And jagg'd his seamlesse coat, had that been fine,
    With curious questions and divisions?

But all the doctrine, which he taught and gave,
    Was cleare as heav'n, from whence it came.
At least those beams of truth, which onely save,
    Surpasse in brightnesse any flame.

*Love God, and love your neighbour. Watch and pray.*
    *Do as ye would be done unto.*
O dark instructions; ev'n as dark as day!
    Who can these Gordian knots undo?

But he doth bid us take his bloud for wine.
    Bid what he please; yet I am sure,
To take and taste what he doth there designe,
    Is all that saves, and not obscure.

Then burn thy Epicycles, foolish man;
    Break all thy spheres, and save thy head.
Faith needs no staffe of flesh, but stoutly can
    To heav'n alone both go, and leade.

*Epicycle*, technical term in Ptolemaic system of astronomy

## The Discharge

Busie enquiring heart, what wouldst thou know?
                Why dost thou prie,
And turn, and leer, and with a licorous eye
                Look high and low;
    And in thy lookings stretch and grow?

Hast thou not made thy counts, and summ'd up all?
                Did not thy heart
Give up the whole, and with the whole depart?
                Let what will fall:
    That which is past who can recall?

Thy life is Gods, thy time to come is gone,
                And is his right.
He is thy night at noon: he is at night
                Thy noon alone.
    The crop is his, for he hath sown.

And well it was for thee, when this befell,
                That God did make
Thy businesse his, and in thy life partake:
                For thou canst tell,
    If it be his once, all is well.

Onely the present is thy part and fee.
                And happy thou,
If, though thou didst not beat thy future brow,
                Thou couldst well see
    What present things requir'd of thee.

*licorous*, greedy for something pleasant, lecherous

They ask enough; why shouldst thou further go?
                              Raise not the mudde
Of future depths, but drink the cleare and good.
                              Dig not for wo
    In times to come; for it will grow.

Man and the present fit: if he provide,
                              He breaks the square.
This houre is mine: if for the next I care,
                              I grow too wide,
    And do encroach upon deaths side.

For death each houre environs and surrounds.
                              He that would know
And care for future chances, cannot go
                              Unto those grounds,
    But through a Church-yard which them bounds.

Things present shrink and die: but they that spend
                              Their thoughts and sense
On future grief, do not remove it thence,
                              But it extend,
    And draw the bottome out an end.

God chains the dog till night: wilt loose the chain,
                              And wake thy sorrow?
Wilt thou forestall it, and now grieve to morrow,
                              And then again
    Grieve over freshly all thy pain?

Either grief will not come: or if it must,
                              Do not forecast.
And while it cometh, it is almost past.
                              Always distrust:
    My God hath promis'd; he is just.

*draw the bottome out an end*, unravel a skein of thread

# Praise

King of Glorie, King of Peace,
    I will love thee:
And that love may never cease,
    I will move thee.

Thou hast granted my request,
    Thou hast heard me:
Thou didst note my working breast,
    Thou hast spar'd me.

Wherefore with my utmost art
    I will sing thee,
And the cream of all my heart
    I will bring thee.

Though my sinnes against me cried,
    Thou didst cleare me;
And alone, when they replied,
    Thou didst heare me.

Sev'n whole dayes, not one in seven,
    I will praise thee.
In my heart, though not in heaven,
    I can raise thee.

Thou grew'st soft and moist with tears,
    Thou relentedst:
And when Justice call'd for fears,
    Thou dissentedst.

Small it is, in this poore sort
    To enroll thee:
Ev'n eternitie is too short
    To extoll thee.

# The Collar

I struck the board, and cry'd, No more.
                    I will abroad.
        What? shall I ever sigh and pine?
My lines and life are free; free as the rode,
        Loose as the winde, as large as store.
                Shall I be still in suit?
        Have I no harvest but a thorn
        To let me bloud, and not restore
    What I have lost with cordiall fruit?
                    Sure there was wine
Before my sighs did drie it: there was corn
            Before my tears did drown it.
        Is the yeare onely lost to me?
                Have I no bayes to crown it?
No flowers, no garlands gay? all blasted?
                    All wasted?
        Not so, my heart: but there is fruit,
                And thou hast hands.
        Recover all thy sigh-blown age
On double pleasures: leave thy cold dispute
Of what is fit, and not. Forsake thy cage,
                Thy rope of sands,
Which pettie thoughts have made, and made to thee
        Good cable, to enforce and draw,
                And be thy law,
        While thou didst wink and wouldst not see.
                Away; take heed:
                I will abroad.
Call in thy deaths head there: tie up thy fears.
                He that forbears
            To suit and serve his need,
                Deserves his load.
But as I rav'd and grew more fierce and wilde
                At every word,
    Me thoughts I heard one calling, *Child!*
            And I reply'd, *My Lord.*

## The Glimpse

       Whither away delight?
Thou cam'st but now: wilt thou so soon depart,
        And give me up to night?
For many weeks of lingring pain and smart
But one half houre of comfort to my heart?

       Me thinks delight should have
More skill in musick, and keep better time.
        Wert thou a winde or wave,
They quickly go and come with lesser crime:
Flowers look about, and die not in their prime.

       Thy short abode and stay
Feeds not, but addes to the desire of meat.
        Lime begg'd of old, they say,
A neighbour spring to cool his inward heat;
Which by the springs accesse grew much more great.

       In hope of thee my heart
Pickt here and there a crumme, and would not die;
        But constant to his part,
When as my fears foretold this, did replie,
A slender thread a gentle guest will tie.

       Yet if the heart that wept
Must let thee go, return when it doth knock.
        Although thy heap be kept
For future times, the droppings of the stock
May oft break forth, and never break the lock.

       If I have more to spinne,
The wheel shall go, so that thy stay be short.
        Thou knowst how grief and sinne
Disturb the work. O make me not their sport,
Who by thy coming may be made a court!

## The Call

Come, my Way, my Truth, my Life:
Such a Way, as gives us breath:
Such a Truth, as ends all strife:
Such a Life, as killeth death.

Come, my Light, my Feast, my Strength:
Such a Light, as shows a feast:
Such a Feast, as mends in length:
Such a Strength, as makes his guest.

Come, my Joy, my Love, my Heart:
Such a Joy, as none can move:
Such a Love, as none can part:
Such a Heart, as joyes in love.

## The Pulley

    When God at first made man,
Having a glasse of blessings standing by;
Let us (said he) poure on him all we can:
Let the worlds riches, which dispersed lie,
        Contract into a span.

    So strength first made a way;
Then beautie flow'd, then wisdome, honour, pleasure:
When almost all was out, God made a stay,
Perceiving that alone of all his treasure
        Rest in the bottome lay.

    For if I should (said he)
Bestow this jewell also on my creature,
He would adore my gifts in stead of me,
And rest in Nature, not the God of Nature:
        So both should losers be.

    Yet let him keep the rest,
But keep them with repining restlesnesse:
Let him be rich and wearie, that at least,
If goodnesse leade him not, yet wearinesse
        May tosse him to my breast.

## The Priesthood

Blest Order, which in power dost so excell,
That with th' one hand thou liftest to the sky,
And with the other throwest down to hell
In thy just censures; fain would I draw nigh,
Fain put thee on, exchanging my lay-sword
            For that of th' holy Word.

But thou art fire, sacred and hallow'd fire;
And I but earth and clay: should I presume
To wear thy habit, the severe attire
My slender compositions might consume.
I am both foul and brittle; much unfit
            To deal in holy Writ.

Yet have I often seen, by cunning hand
And force of fire, what curious things are made
Of wretched earth. Where once I scorn'd to stand,
That earth is fitted by the fire and trade
Of skilfull artists, for the boards of those
            Who make the bravest shows.

But since those great ones, be they ne're so great,
Come from the earth, from whence those vessels come;
So that at once both feeder, dish, and meat
Have one beginning and one finall summe:
I do not greatly wonder at the sight,
            If earth in earth delight.

But th' holy men of God such vessels are,
As serve him up, who all the world commands:
When God vouchsafeth to become our fare,
Their hands convey him, who conveys their hands.
O what pure things, most pure must those things be,
            Who bring my God to me!

Wherefore I dare not, I, put forth my hand
To hold the Ark, although it seem to shake
Through th' old sinnes and new doctrines of our land.
Onely, since God doth often vessels make
Of lowly matter for high uses meet,
               I throw me at his feet.

There will I lie, untill my Maker seek
For some mean stuffe whereon to show his skill:
Then is my time. The distance of the meek
Doth flatter power. Lest good come short of ill
In praising might, the poore do by submission
               What pride by opposition.

## The Search

Whither, O, whither art thou fled,
      My Lord, my Love?
My searches are my daily bread;
      Yet never prove.

My knees pierce th' earth, mine eies the skie;
      And yet the sphere
And centre both to me denie
      That thou art there.

Yet can I mark how herbs below
      Grow green and gay,
As if to meet thee they did know,
      While I decay.

Yet can I mark how starres above
      Simper and shine,
As having keyes unto thy love,
      While poore I pine.

I sent a sigh to seek thee out,
      Deep drawn in pain,
Wing'd like an arrow: but my scout
      Returns in vain.

I tun'd another (having store)
      Into a grone;
Because the search was dumbe before:
      But all was one.

Lord, dost thou some new fabrick mould,
      Which favour winnes,
And keeps thee present, leaving th' old
      Unto their sinnes?

Where is my God? what hidden place
              Conceals thee still?
What covert dare eclipse thy face?
              Is it thy will?

O let not that of any thing;
              Let rather brasse,
Or steel, or mountains be thy ring,
              And I will passe.

Thy will such an intrenching is,
              As passeth thought:
To it all strength, all subtilties
              Are things of nought.

Thy will such a strange distance is,
              As that to it
East and West touch, the poles do kisse,
              And parallels meet.

Since then my grief must be as large,
              As is thy space,
Thy distance from me; see my charge,
              Lord, see my case.

O take these barres, these lengths away;
              Turn, and restore me:
Be not Almightie, let me say,
              Against, but for me;

When thou dost turn, and wilt be neare;
              What edge so keen,
What point so piercing can appeare
              To come between?

>    For as thy absence doth excell
>         All distance known:
>    So doth thy nearenesse bear the bell,
>         Making two one.

*bear the bell*, take first place

# Grief

O who will give me tears? Come all ye springs,
Dwell in my head & eyes: come clouds, & rain:
My grief hath need of all the watry things,
That nature hath produc'd. Let ev'ry vein
Suck up a river to supply mine eyes,
My weary weeping eyes, too drie for me,
Unlesse they get new conduits, new supplies
To bear them out, and with my state agree.
What are two shallow foords, two little spouts
Of a lesse world? the greater is but small,
A narrow cupboard for my griefs and doubts,
Which want provision in the midst of all.
Verses, ye are too fine a thing, too wise
For my rough sorrows: cease, be dumbe and mute,
Give up your feet and running to mine eyes,
And keep your measures for some lovers lute,
Whose grief allows him musick and a ryme:
For mine excludes both measure, tune, and time.
                        Alas, my God!

## The Crosse

       What is this strange and uncouth thing?
To make me sigh, and seek, and faint, and die,
Untill I had some place, where I might sing,
          And serve thee; and not onely I,
But all my wealth and familie might combine
To set thy honour up, as our designe.

       And then when after much delay,
Much wrastling, many a combate, this deare end,
So much desir'd, is giv'n, to take away
          My power to serve thee; to unbend
All my abilities, my designes confound,
And lay my threatnings bleeding on the ground.

       One ague dwelleth in my bones,
Another in my soul (the memorie
What I would do for thee, if once my grones
          Could be allow'd for harmonie):
I am in all a weak disabled thing,
Save in the sight thereof, where strength doth sting.

       Besides, things sort not to my will,
Ev'n when my will doth studie thy renown:
Thou turnest th' edge of all things on me still
          Taking me up to throw me down:
So that, ev'n when my hopes seem to be sped,
I am to grief alive, to them as dead.

       To have my aim, and yet to be
Further from it then when I bent my bow;
To make my hopes my torture, and the fee
          Of all my woes another wo,
Is in the midst of delicates to need,
And ev'n in Paradise to be a weed.

*wrastling*, wrestling; *sped*, fulfilled; *delicates*, luxuries

> Ah my deare Father, ease my smart!
> These contrarieties crush me: these crosse actions
> Doe winde a rope about, and cut my heart:
> > And yet since these thy contradictions
> Are properly a crosse felt by thy Sonne,
> With but foure words, my words, *Thy will be done.*

## The Flower

How fresh, O Lord, how sweet and clean
Are thy returns! ev'n as the flowers in spring;
    To which, besides their own demean,
The late-past frosts tributes of pleasure bring.
        Grief melts away
        Like snow in May,
As if there were no such cold thing.

Who would have thought my shrivel'd heart
Could have recover'd greennesse? It was gone
    Quite under ground; as flowers depart
To see their mother-root, when they have blown;
        Where they together
        All the hard weather,
Dead to the world, keep house unknown.

These are thy wonders, Lord of power,
Killing and quickning, bringing down to hell
    And up to heaven in an houre;
Making a chiming of a passing-bell.
        We say amisse,
        This or that is:
Thy word is all, if we could spell.

O that I once past changing were,
Fast in thy Paradise, where no flower can wither!
    Many a spring I shoot up fair,
Offring at heav'n, growing and groning thither:
        Nor doth my flower
        Want a spring-showre,
My sinnes and I joining together.

*demean*, bearing (demeanour) and estate (demesne)

But while I grow in a straight line,
Still upwards bent, as if heav'n were mine own,
    Thy anger comes, and I decline:
What frost to that? what pole is not the zone,
        Where all things burn,
        When thou dost turn,
    And the least frown of thine is shown?

    And now in age I bud again,
After so many deaths I live and write;
    I once more smell the dew and rain,
And relish versing: O my onely light,
        It cannot be
        That I am he
    On whom thy tempests fell all night.

    These are thy wonders, Lord of love,
To make us see we are but flowers that glide:
    Which when we once can finde and prove
Thou hast a garden for us, where to bide.
        Who would be more,
        Swelling through store,
    Forfeit their Paradise by their pride.

---

*glide*, slip away

## The Sonne

Let forrain nations of their language boast,
What fine varietie each tongue affords:
I like our language, as our men and coast:
Who cannot dresse it well, want wit, not words.
How neatly doe we give one onely name
To parents issue and the sunnes bright starre!
A sonne is light and fruit; a fruitfull flame
Chasing the fathers dimnesse, carri'd farre
From the first man in th' East, to fresh and new
Western discov'ries of posteritie.
So in one word our Lords humilitie
We turn upon him in a sense most true:
    For what Christ once in humblenesse began,
    We him in glorie call, *The Sonne of Man.*

*coast*, region, country

## A True Hymne

      My joy, my life, my crown!
My heart was meaning all the day,
        Somewhat it fain would say:
And still it runneth mutt'ring up and down
With onely this, *My joy, my life, my crown.*

      Yet slight not these few words:
If truly said, they may take part
        Among the best in art.
The finenesse which a hymne or psalme affords,
Is, when the soul unto the lines accords.

      He who craves all the minde,
And all the soul, and strength, and time,
        If the words onely ryme,
Justly complains, that somewhat is behinde
To make his verse, or write a hymne in kinde.

      Whereas if th' heart be moved,
Although the verse be somewhat scant,
        God doth supplie the want.
As when th' heart sayes (sighing to be approved)
*O, could I love!* and stops: God writeth, *Loved.*

---

*behinde*, lacking

## Bitter-sweet

Ah my deare angrie Lord,
Since thou dost love, yet strike;
Cast down, yet help afford;
Sure I will do the like.

I will complain, yet praise;
I will bewail, approve:
And all my sowre-sweet dayes
I will lament, and love.

## The Glance

    When first thy sweet and gracious eye
Vouchsaf'd ev'n in the midst of youth and night
To look upon me, who before did lie
          Weltring in sinne;
    I felt a sugred strange delight,
Passing all cordials made by any art
Bedew, embalme, and overrunne my heart,
          And take it in.

    Since that time many a bitter storm
My soul hath felt, ev'n able to destroy,
Had the malicious and ill-meaning harm
          His swing and sway:
    But still thy sweet originall joy,
Sprung from thine eye, did work within my soul,
And surging griefs, when they grew bold, controll,
          And got the day.

    If thy first glance so powerfull be,
A mirth but open'd and seal'd up again;
What wonders shall we feel, when we shall see
          Thy full-ey'd love!
    When thou shalt look us out of pain,
And one aspect of thine spend in delight
More then a thousand sunnes disburse in light,
          In heav'n above.

## The Forerunners

The harbingers are come. See, see their mark;
White is their colour, and behold my head.
But must they have my brain? must they dispark
Those sparkling notions, which therein were bred?
      Must dulnesse turn me to a clod?
Yet have they left me, *Thou art still my God*.

Good men ye be, to leave me my best room,
Ev'n all my heart, and what is lodged there:
I passe not, I, what of the rest become,
So *Thou art still my God*, be out of fear.
      He will be pleased with that dittie;
And if I please him, I write fine and wittie.

Farewell sweet phrases, lovely metaphors.
But will ye leave me thus? when ye before
Of stews and brothels onely knew the doores,
Then did I wash you with my tears, and more,
      Brought you to Church well drest and clad:
My God must have my best, ev'n all I had.

Lovely enchanting language, sugar-cane,
Hony of roses, whither wilt thou flie?
Hath some fond lover tic'd thee to thy bane?
And wilt thou leave the Church, and love a stie?
      Fie, thou wilt soil thy broider'd coat,
And hurt thy self, and him that sings the note.

Let foolish lovers, if they will love dung,
With canvas, not with arras, clothe their shame:
Let follie speak in her own native tongue.
True beautie dwells on high: ours is a flame
      But borrow'd thence to light us thither.
Beautie and beauteous words should go together.

*dispark*, disperse

Yet if you go, I passe not; take your way:
For, *Thou art still my God*, is all that ye
Perhaps with more embellishment can say.
Go birds of spring: let winter have his fee;
      Let a bleak palenesse chalk the doore,
So all within be livelier then before.

## The Invitation

Come ye hither All, whose taste
                Is your waste;
Save your cost, and mend your fare.
God is here prepar'd and drest,
                And the feast,
God, in whom all dainties are.

Come ye hither All, whom wine
                Doth define,
Naming you not to your good:
Weep what ye have drunk amisse,
                And drink this,
Which before ye drink is bloud.

Come ye hither All, whom pain
                Doth arraigne,
Bringing all your sinnes to sight:
Taste and fear not: God is here
                In this cheer,
And on sinne doth cast the fright.

Come ye hither All, whom joy
                Doth destroy,
While ye graze without your bounds:
Here is joy that drowneth quite
                Your delight,
As a floud the lower grounds.

Come ye hither All, whose love
                Is your dove,
And exalts you to the skie:
Here is love, which having breath
                Ev'n in death.
After death can never die.

Lord I have invited all,
                       And I shall
Still invite, still call to thee:
For it seems but just and right
                       In my sight,
Where is All, there All should be.

## The Elixir

Teach me, my God and King,
 In all things thee to see,
And what I do in any thing,
 To do it as for thee:

Not rudely, as a beast,
 To runne into an action;
But still to make thee prepossest,
 And give it his perfection.

A man that looks on glasse,
 On it may stay his eye;
Or if he pleaseth, through it passe,
 And then the heav'n espie.

All may of thee partake:
 Nothing can be so mean,
Which with his tincture (for thy sake)
 Will not grow bright and clean.

A servant with this clause
 Makes drudgerie divine:
Who sweeps a room, as for thy laws,
 Makes that and th' action fine.

This is the famous stone
 That turneth all to gold:
For that which God doth touch and own
 Cannot for lesse be told.

*The Elixir*, the philosopher's stone, supposed by alchemists to have the power of turning baser metals into gold; *make thee prepossest*, give thee a prior claim; *tincture*, in alchemy 'a supposed spiritual principle or immaterial substance whose character or quality may be infused into material things' (*OED*)

## A Wreath

A wreathed garland of deserved praise,
Of praise deserved, unto thee I give,
I give to thee, who knowest all my wayes,
My crooked winding wayes, wherein I live,
Wherein I die, not live: for life is straight,
Straight as a line, and ever tends to thee,
To thee, who art more farre above deceit,
Then deceit seems above simplicitie.
Give me simplicitie, that I may live,
So live and like, that I may know, thy wayes,
Know them and practise them: then shall I give
For this poore wreath, give thee a crown of praise.

## Judgement

Almightie Judge, how shall poore wretches brook
                Thy dreadfull look,
Able a heart of iron to appall,
                      When thou shalt call
        For ev'ry mans peculiar book?

What others mean to do, I know not well;
                Yet I heare tell,
That some will turn thee to some leaves therein
                So void of sinne,
        That they in merit shall excell.

But I resolve, when thou shalt call for mine,
                That to decline,
And thrust a Testament into thy hand:
                  Let that be scann'd.
        There thou shalt finde my faults are thine.

## Heaven

O who will show me those delights on high?
    *Echo.*  I.
Thou Echo, thou art mortall, all men know.
    *Echo.*  No.
Wert thou not born among the trees and leaves?
    *Echo.*  Leaves.
And are there any leaves, that still abide?
    *Echo.*  Bide.
What leaves are they? impart the matter wholly.
    *Echo.*  Holy.
Are holy leaves the Echo then of blisse?
    *Echo.*  Yes.
Then tell me, what is that supreme delight?
    *Echo.*  Light.
Light to the minde: what shall the will enjoy?
    *Echo.*  Joy.
But are there cares and businesse with the pleasure?
    *Echo.*  Leisure.
Light, joy, and leisure; but shall they persever?
    *Echo.*  Ever.

*persever*, 'Of things: to continue, last, endure – 1696' (*OED*)

## Love

Love bade me welcome: yet my soul drew back,
    Guiltie of dust and sinne.
But quick-ey'd Love, observing me grow slack
    From my first entrance in,
Drew nearer to me, sweetly questioning,
    If I lack'd any thing.

A guest, I answer'd, worthy to be here:
    Love said, You shall be he.
I the unkinde, ungratefull? Ah my deare,
    I cannot look on thee.
Love took my hand, and smiling did reply,
    Who made the eyes but I?

Truth Lord, but I have marr'd them: let my shame
    Go where it doth deserve.
And know you not, sayes Love, who bore the blame?
    My deare, then I will serve.
You must sit down, sayes Love, and taste my meat;
    So I did sit and eat.

# From *A Priest to the Temple* or *The Country Parson*

## The Parson praying

The Countrey Parson, when he is to read divine services, composeth himselfe to all possible reverence; lifting up his heart and hands, and eyes, and using all other gestures which may express a hearty, and unfeyned devotion. This he doth, first, as being truly touched and amazed with the Majesty of God, before whom he then presents himself; yet not as himself alone, but as presenting with himself the whole Congregation, whose sins he then beares, and brings with his own to the heavenly altar to be bathed, and washed in the sacred Laver of Christs blood. Secondly, as this is the true reason of his inward feare, so he is content to expresse this outwardly to the utmost of his power; that being first affected himself, hee may affect also his people, knowing that no Sermon moves them so much to a reverence, which they forget againe, when they come to pray, as a devout behaviour in the very act of praying. Accordingly his voyce is humble, his words treatable, and slow; yet not so slow neither, as to let the fervency of the supplicant hang and dy between speaking, but with a grave livelinesse, between feare and zeal, pausing yet pressing, he performes his duty. Besides his example, he having often instructed his people how to carry themselves in divine service, exacts of them all possible reverence, by no means enduring either talking, or sleeping, or gazing, or leaning, or halfe-kneeling, or any undutifull behaviour in them, but causing them, when they sit, or stand, or kneel, to do all in a strait, and steady posture, as attending to what is done in the Church, and every one, man, and child, answering aloud both Amen, and all other answers, which are on the Clerks and peoples part to answer; which answers also are to be done not in a hudling, or slubbering fashion, gaping, or scratching the head, or spitting even in the midst of their answer, but gently and pausably, thinking what they say; so that while they answer, *As it was in the beginning*, &c. they meditate as they speak, that God hath ever had his people, that have glorified him as wel as now, and that he shall have so for ever. And the like in other answers. This is that which the Apostle cals a reasonable service, *Rom*. 12. when we speak not as Parrats, without reason, or offer up such sacrifices as they did of old, which was of beasts devoyd of reason; but when we use our reason, and apply our powers to the service of him, that gives them. If there be any of the gentry or nobility of the Parish, who somtimes make it a piece of state not to come at the beginning of service with their poor neighbours, but at mid-prayers, both to their own loss, and of theirs also who gaze upon them when they come in, and neglect the present service of God, he by no means suffers it, but after divers gentle admonitions, if they persevere, he causes them to be presented: or if the poor Church-wardens be affrighted with their greatness, notwithstanding his instruction that they ought not to be so, but even to let the world sinke, so they do their duty; he presents them himself, only protesting to them, that not any ill will draws him to it, but the debt and obligation of his calling, being to obey God rather then men.

*Poem not included in Herbert's selection for* The Temple

## The Holy Communion (2)

O gratious Lord, how shall I know
Whether in these gifts thou bee so
    As thou art evry-where;
Or rather so, as thou alone
Tak'st all the Lodging, leaving none
    ffor thy poore creature there?

ffirst I am sure, whether bread stay
Or whether Bread doe fly away
    Concerneth bread, not mee.
But that both thou and all thy traine
Bee there, to thy truth, & my gaine,
    Concerneth mee & Thee.

And if in comming to thy foes
Thou dost come first to them, that showes
    The hast of thy good will.
Or if that thou two stations makest
In Bread & mee, the way thou takest
    Is more, but for mee still.

Then of this also I am sure
That thou didst all those pains endure
    To' abolish Sinn, not Wheat.
Creatures are good, & have their place;
Sinn onely, which did all deface,
    Thou drivest from his seat.

*hast*, haste

I could beleeue an Impanation
At the rate of an Incarnation,
    If thou hadst dyde for Bread.
But that which made my soule to dye,
My flesh, & fleshly villany,
    That allso made thee dead.

That fflesh is there, mine eyes deny:
And what shold flesh but flesh discry,
    The noblest sence of five?
If glorious bodies pass the sight,
Shall they be food & strength & might
    Euen there, where they deceiue?

Into my soule this cannot pass;
fflesh (though exalted) keeps his grass
    And cannot turn to soule.
Bodyes & Minds are different Spheres
Nor can they change their bounds & meres,
    But keep a constant Pole.

This gift of all gifts is the best,
Thy flesh the least that I request.
    Thou took'st that pledg from mee:
Give me not that I had before,
Or give mee that, so I have more;
    My God, give mee all Thee.

*Impanation,* 'in eucharistic theory: a local presence or inclusion of the body of Christ in the bread after consecration: one of the modifications of the doctrine of the real presence' (*OED*)

## Letter to Sir Henry Herbert

Dear Bro;

That you did not only entertain my proposals, but advance them, was lovingly done, and like a good brother. Yet truly it was none of my meaning, when I wrote, to putt one of our neeces into your hands but barely what I wrote I meant, and no more; and am glad that although you offer more, yet you will doe, as you write, that alsoe. I was desirous to putt a good mind into the way of charity, and that was all I intended. For concerning your offer of receiving one, I will tell you what I wrote to our eldest brother, when he urged one upon me, and but one, and that at my choice. I wrote to him that I would have both or neither; and that upon this ground, because they were to come into an unknown country, tender in knowledge, sense, and age, and knew none but one who could be no company to them. Therefore I considered that if one only came, the comfort intended would prove a discomfort. Since that I have seen the fruit of my observation; for they have lived so lovingly, lying, eating, walking, praying, working, still together, that I take a comfort therein; and would not have to part them yet, till I take some opportunity to let them know your love, for which both they shall, and I doe, thank you. It is true there is a third sister, whom to receive were the greatest charitie of all, for she is youngest, and least looked unto; having none to doe it but her school-mistresse, and you know what those mercenary creatures are. Neither hath she any to repair unto at good times, as Christmas, &c. which, you know, is the encouragement of learning all the year after, except my cousin Bett take pitty of her, which yet at that distance is some difficulty. If you could think of taking her, as once you did, surely it were a great good deed, and I would have her conveyed to you. But I judge you not: doe that which GOD shall put into your hart, and the LORD bless all your purposes to his glory. Yet, truly if you take her not, I am thinking to do it, even beyond my strengthe; especially at this time, being more beggarly now than I have been these many years, as having spent two hundred pounds in building; which to me that have nothing yett, is very much. But though I both consider this, and your observation, also, of the unthankfulness of kindred bredd up, (which generally is very true,) yet I care not; I forgett all thinges, so I may doe them good who want it. So I doe my part to them, lett them think of me what they will or can. I have another judge, to whom I stand or fall. Yf I should regard such things, it were in another's power to defeat my charity, and evill shold be stronger then good: but difficulties are so farr from cooling christians, that they whett them. Truly it grieves me to think of the child, how destitute she is, and that in this necessary time of education. For the time of breeding is the time of doing children good; and not as many who think they have done fairly, if they leave them a good portion after their decease. But take this rule, and it is an outlandish one, which I commend to you as being now a father, 'the best-bredd child hath the best portion'. Well; the good GOD bless you more and more; and all yours; and make your family, a housefull of GOD's servants. So prayes

Your ever loving brother,

G. HERBERT.

My wife's and neeces' service.

    To my very dear brother
    Sir Henry Herbert, at Court.
       [? Autumn, 1630]

## A Selection from *Outlandish Proverbs*

These are taken from Herbert's collection of more than 1,000 foreign proverbs, published in 1640 as *Outlandish Proverbs selected by Mr GH*.

3. A handfull of good life is better then a bushell of learning.

4. He that studies his content, wants it.

10. All is well with him, who is beloved of his neighbours.

49. Love and a Cough cannot be hid.

62. A cherefull looke makes a dish a feast.

80. He that is warme, thinkes all so.

120. Keepe good men company, and you shall be of the number.

130. The Fox, when hee cannot reach the grapes, saies they are not ripe.

141. Love your neighbour, yet pull not downe your hedge.

143. A drunkards purse is a bottle.

178. Thinke of ease, but worke on.

196. Whose house is of glasse, must not throw stones at another.

199. I wept when I was borne, and every day shewes why.

236. Advise none to marry or to goe to warre.

248. Knowledge is folly, except grace guide it.

286. Chuse not an house nere an Inne (viz. for noise) or in a corner (for filth).

290. Goe not for every griefe to the Physitian, nor for every quarrell to the Lawyer, nor for every thirst to the pot.

317. No lock will hold against the power of gold.

343. Hee that lies with the dogs, riseth with fleas.

395. To a crazy ship all winds are contrary.

401. Love is not found in the market.

408. An ill labourer quarrells with his tooles.

416. He that seekes trouble never misses.

417. He that once deceives is ever suspected.

456. Good finds good.

460. The first degree of folly is to hold oneself wise, the second to professe it, the third to despise counsell.

504. When children stand quiet, they have done some ill.

510. If the wise erred not, it would goe hard with fooles.

524. Living well is the best revenge.

540. Love is the true price of love.

548. Faire words make mee looke to my purse.

580. Good & quickly seldom meet.

626. Skill and confidence are an unconquered army.

631. To bee beloved is above all bargaines.

646. Love makes one fitt for any work.

682. More have repented speech than silence.

724. Be what thou wouldst seeme to be.

733. Where there is peace, God is.

781. He that feares death lives not.

784. He that marries for wealth sells his liberty.

806. An ill deede cannot bring honour.

808. All are not merry that dance lightly.

828. Better a snotty child, then his nose wip'd off.

865. The Rich knows not who is his friend.

882. One houres sleep before midnight is worth three after.

897. Hee hath no leisure who useth it not.

907. Halfe the world knows not how the other halfe lives.

924. The Chollerick drinkes, the Melancholick eates, the Flegmatick sleepes.

929. Wine is a turne-coate (first a friend, then an enemy).

937. The dainties of the great are the teares of the poore.

# Select Bibliography

## Editions

F. E. Hutchinson, ed., *The Works of George Herbert*, Oxford University Press, 1941.

Ernest Rhys, ed., *The Temple and A Priest to the Temple by George Herbert, with an introduction by Edward Thomas*, Everyman's Library (Dent) 1908.

Ann Pasternak Slater, ed., *George Herbert: The Complete English Works*, Everyman's Library (David Campbell Ltd), 1995.

John Tobin, ed., *George Herbert: The Complete English Poems*, Penguin, 1991.

## Selections

W. H. Auden, ed., *George Herbert*, Penguin, 1973.

R. S. Thomas, ed., *A Choice of George Herbert's Verse*, Faber, 1967.

## Wider reading

Amy M. Charles, *A Life of George Herbert*, Cornell University Press, 1977.

Julia Carolyn Guernsey, *The Pulse of Praise: Form as a Second Self in the Poetry of George Herbert*, Associated University Presses, 1999.

Kenneth Mason, *George Herbert: Priest and Poet*, SLG Press, 1980.

C. A. Patrides, ed., *George Herbert: The Critical Heritage*, Routledge, 1983.

David Scott, *Sacred Tongues: The Golden Age of Spiritual Writing*, SPCK, 2001.

Joseph H. Summers, *George Herbert: His Religion and Art*, Chatto and Windus, 1954.

Helen Vendler, *The Poetry of George Herbert*, Harvard University Press, 1975.


Note: Izaak Walton's *The Life of Mr George Herbert* (1670) is included in the Slater and Tobin editions. The T. S. Eliot article mentioned in the Introduction can be found in the volume edited by C. A. Patrides.

## Index of First Lines

A broken ALTAR, Lord, thy servant reares  21
Ah my deare angrie Lord  94
Almightie Judge, how shall poore wretches brook  102
As men, for fear the starres should sleep and nod  74
A wreathed garland of deserved praise  101

Blest be the God of love  38
Blest Order, which in power doth so excell  82
Busie enquiring heart, what wouldst thou know?  75

Come, my Way, my Truth, my Life  80
Come ye hither All, whose taste/Is your waste  98

Having been tenant long to a rich Lord  23
Heark, how the birds do sing  69
How fresh, O Lord, how sweet and clean  90
How soon doth man decay!  53

I cannot ope mine eyes  37
I have consider'd it, and finde  22
I joy, deare Mother, when I view  57
I know the wayes of Learning; both the head  49
I made a posie, while the day ran by  52
I strucke the board and cry'd, No more  78
If as a flowre doth spread and die  34
If as the windes and waters here below  71

King of Glorie, King of Peace  77

Let all the world in ev'ry corner sing  33
Let forrain nations of their language boast  92
Listen sweet Dove unto my song  36
Lord, how can man preach thy eternall word?  40
Lord, make me coy and tender to offend:  51
Lord, my first fruits present themselves to thee  1
Lord, who createdst man in wealth and store  25

## Index of First Lines

Lord, who hast form'd me out of mud    41
Lord, with what care hast thou begirt us round!    26
Love bade me welcome: yet my soul drew back    104

Money, thou bane of blisse, & sourse of wo    45
My God, a verse is not a crown    44
My joy, my life, my crown!    93

Not in rich furniture, or fine aray    31

O gratious Lord, how shall I know    107
O sacred Providence, who from end to end    60
O who will give me tears? come all ye springs    87
O who will show me those delights on high?    103
Oh glorious spirits, who after all your bands    46
Oh that I knew how all thy lights combine    35

Peace mutt'ring thoughts, and do not grudge to keep    42
Peace pratler, do not lowre    56
Poore heart, lament    72
Prayer the Churches banquet, Angels age    30

Rise heart; thy Lord is risen. Sing his praise    24

Sorrie I am, my God, sorrie I am    66
Sweet day, so cool, so calm, so bright    48
Sweet Peace, where dost thou dwell? I humbly crave    67
Sweetest of sweets, I thank you: when displeasure    39
Sweetest Saviour, if my soul    59

Teach me, my God and King    100
The harbingers are come. See, see their mark    96
The merrie world did on a day    58
Thou, whose sweet youth and early hopes inhance    2

What is this strange and uncouth thing?    88
When first my lines of heav'nly joyes made mention    55
When first thou didst entice to thee my heart    27
When first thy sweet and gracious eye    95
When God at first made man    81
When my devotions could not pierce/Thy silent eares    47
Whither away delight?    79
Whither, O, whither art thou fled    84